dB**XL**™
To Go

10 Ready-to-run Programs to Computerize your Business

Peter G. Randall
Steven J. Bennett

Simon & Schuster, Inc.
Gulf+Western Building
One Gulf+Western Plaza
New York, NY 10023

Manufactured in the United States of America

4 5 6 7 8 9 10

Library of Congress Cataloging-in-Publication Data

Randall, Peter G. 1951-

dBXL To Go [computer file].

1 computer disk; 5 1/4 in. = reference manual. System requirements: IBM PC, XT, AT, or other compatibles; 512K PC DOS 2.0 or MS DOS 2.1 or higher; dBXL ; 2 Disk drives; printer with condense print capability.

Summary: provides twenty ready-to-run user applications for dBXL and programming utilities for advanced dBXL users.

1. Data base management—Software.

2. Business Software.

I. Bennett, Steven J., 1951-

II. dBXL (computer program)

III. Title QA76.9.D3R25 1989   005.75'65   87-7089

ISBN 0-13-196214-0

012-003-099

Contents

Acknowledgments

We'd first off like to express our appreciation and gratitude to Terry Anderson for helping us conceive and refine this book project, and to Joe Esposito for his ongoing support. Thanks also to our colleagues who reviewed the manuscript and the programs, Bob Moran, Peter K. Kinder, Alan Wichlei, and Alan Muster. Hats off to Nancy MacDonald for helping us assemble the documentation.

Special appreciation goes to Alex Randall, who introduced us—without him, this book never would have come about. Finally, we thank our friends and families for their patience and understanding while we wrote the book.

Trademarks

dBXL is a registered trademark of WordTech Systems, Inc.. Epson is a registered trademark of Epson Corporation. IBM PC and IBM are registered trademarks of International Business Machines, Inc. WordStar is a registered trademark of MicroPro. Quicksilver is a trademark licensed to WordTech Systems, Inc. by Quicksilver Software, Inc. Compaq is a trademark of Compaq Computer Corporation. PC Magazine is a trademark of Ziff Communications Co. All product names mentioned in this manual and not listed above are the trademarks of their respective companies.

Read This First

Beginning dBXL users: Carefully read the System Checklist, the Introduction, and Chapter 1 before attempting to use any of the programs in this book. Also, you are urged to read the *Getting Started* booklet supplied by WordTech Systems, Inc. with your dBXL program, and to work through the dBXL tutorial, also supplied by WordTech Systems, Inc.

Intermediate dBXL users: Skim the introduction, and read Chapter 1 before proceeding.

Advanced dBXL users: Read Quick Start before running any of the dBXL programs; even if you're a dBXL pro, the information provided in Quick Start will save you a lot of time and guessing. You should also scan the basic setup options described in Chapter 1.

System Checklist

To run any of the dBXL To Go programs provided on the diskettes attached to the back cover of this book, you will need the following:

1. A copy of dBXL

2. An IBM PC, XT, AT, or 100-percent compatible computer with at least 430 kilobytes of RAM.

3. A printer capable of condensed (15 characters-per-inch or smaller) print in addition to normal size print, or a wide carriage printer capable of printing 132 columns.

It is assumed that before you begin using any of the programs in this book, you have installed dBXL on your computer. If not, read through the installation information supplied by WordTech Systems, Inc. and make sure that dBXL is operational and ready to run.

Introduction

dBXL is one of the most powerful microcomputer programs available today. You can use it to create sophisticated applications for just about all your information management needs. But to use dBXL, you must learn a complex programming language and set aside a fair amount of time—even if you use the program's built-in menu system, INTRO.

This book will give you a different kind of INTRO-style instant productivity, with the programs and utilities on the diskettes in the back cover. You'll find 10 powerful programs that will help you with many common business needs, including:

Address Book Program. An electronic address book that keeps track of personal and business contracts, and prints out mailing labels, reports and standard Rolodex-type cards.

Invoice Program. A general purpose billing program designed for retail or service businesses. Generates invoices, accounts receivable reports, and other valuable printouts.

Dynamic Inventory Management Program. Tracks inventory purchases and compares them against sales, and calculates on-hand balance. Generates customer, supplier, and part number reports for all or selected transactions.

Note Card Program. An all-purpose electronic index card system. User can input unlimited notes using the dBXL text editor. Note cards can be retrieved and organized by user-defined codes.

Mailing List Management Program. Comprehensive system for inputting mailing label information and creating custom lists. Sophisticated user-defined coding system. Outputs labels in most common standard formats.

Time Billing Program. Complete professional system for recording billable time on electronic time sheets. Comprehensive invoicing and invoice tracking system generates client bills and a variety of valuable management reports.

Travel Expense Reporting Program. Tracks travel expenses and totals company-paid expenses versus traveler's out-of-pocket expenses. Generates report by traveler, client, department, or budget center.

Sales Lead Management Program. Flexible system for tracking sales leads from a variety of marketing sources. Provides valuable information regarding lead sources. Outputs lists of leads to be followed up by appropriate sales reps.

Bibliography Program. Complete system for creating bibliographic and reference lists in standard format. Key word search and other useful features for locating and organizing records. Allows for unlimited length abstracts.

*Capital Assets Tracking Program*ry. Catalogs capital assets and calculates residual value and depreciation. Generates a number of reports for financial reporting purposes.

In addition to the applications programs, you'll find 10 power utilities. If you are an experienced dBXL programmer, you can use them to enhance and customize you own programs.

dBXL Terms And Concepts

While you don't need to know any dBXL commands to use the programs in this book, you should be familiar with several basic terms and concepts. First, you should understand that a database is simply a collection of information organized in a specific way. An address book, for example, is a database. Each person's name and address entry is a **record,** and the specific entries, such as name, address, city, and so on are **fields.**

An address book is usually organized alphabetically. If everyone's record were placed on a card, as in a Rolodex-type address file, you could reorder them by state, profession, or by any other criteria. That's one of the advantages of an electronic database—you can quickly resort the records any number of ways. This can be easily accomplished with dBXL by using several different indexes that order records according to several different criteria. By switching the index, the file quickly appears to the user as if the data were actually sorted in different ways.

In addition to quickly reordering records, an electronic database also allows you to pull out records that have like attributes (e.g., everyone who lives in Ohio, everyone who has the zip code 02138, etc.) without having to physically rearrange the records. Note: One of the programs you'll find on the diskettes is an electronic address book (see Chapter 2).

Each dBXL To Go program is an electronic database. You create records for the database by selecting the Add Data option from the program's Main Menu (see below). You can later use the program's Scan functions to locate specific records for viewing, editing, or deleting, and the program's Report options to print custom lists of records in the database.

Using dBXL To Go Menus

All programs in this book are menu-driven, which means that you select an option from a menu to carry out functions, such as entering or editing data, generating reports, and using utility functions. To select a menu item, use the up or down arrow keys (8 or 2) on the keypad to position the light bar cursor over the item you want, and then press **<ENTER>**. You can also simply type the number of the item. You do not need to press **<ENTER>**. In some cases, after selecting a menu option, you will be asked to answer **Yes** or **No**. When the action does not have potentially catastrophic consequences if you make a mistake, such as deciding whether you want to output a report to your screen or your printer, you do not need to press **<ENTER>** after entering your choice. Just type **Y** or **N**. In other cases, where you might regret making a choice, such as deleting records, you must press **<ENTER>** after typing **Y** or **N** to confirm your choice.

Entering Data

Input Screens

Generally, when you select a menu item, an input screen will be displayed. (Exceptions are menu options that do not require additional data to be input, such as utility functions that can be executed as soon as you select the option.) An input screen displays all the fields in which you can enter information. The data fields on the input screen are designated by a highlighted **bar** (also called a **reverse video bar**) in which you type numerical or alphabetic characters. The word that describes the field is a **label** (e.g., name, address, city, and state), and appears to the left of or above the input field. The blinking cursor indicates the field in which you are currently inputting information.

Data Entry Format

It is vitally important that you are consistent with your data entry. The reason is that dBXL is case-sensitive, which means it distinguishes between upper- and lower case letters. As a result, if you are inconsistent, the scan routines and reports may not include all the records you expect. For example, let's say you were using the Time Billing Program, and sometimes entered a project code as HAL 5000, and other times at Hal 5000. When you went to seach for or print all records involving HAL 5000, you would miss those entered as Hal 5000. Since it is easy to forget how you entered data a month or two ago, and more than one person might be entering data into the program, each with his or her own conventions, we suggest keeping a list of "official" data entry codes by the computer, along with a set of rules for generating new ones.

Navigation

Whenever an input screen is displayed, the blinking cursor will be in the first field in which you can enter data. Each time you press <ENTER>, the cursor will move to the next field. The following keys are used to enter and edit information within an input screen.

ENTERING/EDITING DATA

<ENTER>. When you have typed the desired information, press <ENTER>, and the cursor will move to the next field. If you want to leave a field blank, press <ENTER> without typing anything.

Tab Keys. The Tab keys move the cursor backward or forward. You can overwrite existing information or modify it with the Delete or Backspace keys (see below). Press <ENTER> when you are done.

Cursor Keys. The Up cursor key moves the cursor backward through the input screen. The left and right cursor keys move the cursor within a field.

Backspace key. Each time you press the Backspace key, one character to the left of the cursor will be deleted in the current field.

Delete key. This key deletes the character above the blinking cursor.

Insert key. This key toggles between insert and typeover mode. When in insert mode, whatever you type will be inserted above the cursor, pushing existing data to the right. In typeover mode, whatever you type will overwrite existing data.

Completing Data Input,
Exiting The Input Screen

When you press <ENTER> in the last field on the screen during data entry, the record will be added to the database. There are two other ways to indicate that a record is complete:

PgDn and PgUp. If you press either of these keys, the record will be entered into the database, regardless of which field is current. This can be useful if you only wish to enter information in the first few fields. If you accidentally press **PgDn** or **PgUp** before you are done entering all the desired information, you will have to select the Edit option from the Main Menu and add the desired information.

CTRL-END. Pressing and holding the **CTRL** key and then pressing the **END** key has the same effect as pressing **PgDn** or **PgUp**. The CTRL-END combination is a more desirable shortcut for adding records to the database, because there is less chance of accidentally invoking it before a record is complete.

ESC. To escape from an input screen without adding the information to the database, press **ESC**. This will return you to the menu.

Exiting From A dBXL To Go Program

It is critical that you exit properly from a dBXL To Go program. The only "legal" way to do so is to select the exit option from the Main Menu. If you merely turn your computer off or soft boot by pressing **CTRL-ALT-DEL**, you will probably damage the index files, and you may damage the database itself. The index files can be repaired by selecting the Reindex option from the Utilities Menu (which is accessed from the Main Menu of each program). If the database is damaged, however, you may have to start from scratch and re-enter the data into a clean copy of the program, or restore the data from your most recent backup.

Anatomy Of A dBXL To Go Program

Each of the ten programs on the distribution diskettes is a complete application package. In the form provided on the distribution diskettes, the programs must be run with dBXL. Note: You can run any of the programs in this book without dBXL if you first compile them, using WordTech Systems Quicksilver compiler.

All dBXL To Go programs consist of the following modules and routines:

1. Data entry module: includes input screens. These are used to enter and select information.

2. Scan/Search routines: locate records for viewing, editing, updating, or deleting.

3. Report generator modules: create reports based on the criteria you select. Most of the report options display an input screen for you to enter your selection criteria.

4. Utility modules: include functions such as reindexing the database, password on/off, report header customization, printer setup, and other actions required by a specific program (e.g., in the Invoicing Program, Chapter 3, the utilities module allows you to specify the sales tax percentage in your state, so proper tax will be automatically calculated each time you generate an invoice.)

How To Use This Book

Each chapter in dBXL To Go is a self-contained manual for the associated program on the enclosed diskettes. Installation and basic setup is the same for all programs, and is explained in Chapter 1. (Chapter 1 also explains certain essential DOS concepts and functions, such as creating a config.sys file and setting the path command.) Before you begin using any of the dBXL To Go programs, browse through the chapter relating to it and familiarize yourself with the layout and terminology of the program.

Saving Your Work

Whether or not you are using a hard disk system, it is vitally important to back up your work frequently. This can save you hours of painful data re-entry. It is only necessary to back up your .dbf files. The other programs can be re-installed from your working diskette. Note: The first time you run a dBXL To Go program, it will create the required index files. Index files have an .ndx extension. Don't bother backing up your .ndx files, since each time a program is run, it checks whether the index files are present. If not, it will create them.

The Next Step

Read Chapter 1 before attempting to use any of the programs provided with this book; it will teach you how to prepare your computer and customize the programs. Then get ready for some instant productivity.

Peter G. Randall

Steven J. Bennett

dBXL™
To Go

1 Installation and Setup

Introduction

This chapter is divided into four sections: DOS setup, hard disk installation, floppy disk installation, and dBXL To Go setup options. Even if you've had some experience with general computing and with dBXL, we recommend that you read the following material carefully before using any of the dBXL To Go programs.

Making A Working Copy Of
The Distribution Diskettes

As with any software package, never use your distribution diskettes as your main copies; floppy disks are easily damaged, and you may find yourself in a frustrating situation should anything happen to the originals.

The dBXL To Go diskette is not copy protected. To make a working copy, take two formatted double-sided, double-density diskettes and copy all the files from the distribution disk, using the DISKCOPY a: b: command. When you are done, put the distribution diskettes in a safe place.

To load dBXL To Go programs on a hard disk, use the batch file provided on disk 1 to copy the dBXL To Go program files into appropriate directories (the procedure for doing this is described in each chapter). We recommend keeping each program in its own directory to simplify operation and backup.

Once you've copied the files for the programs you wish to run, read the sections in the chapters explaining how to start them, then get ready for instant productivity.

DOS Setup

Config.sys

Prior to using dBXL, you must create a **config.sys** file. The config.sys file tells the computer how to allocate available memory. If you boot your system from a floppy disk, the config.sys

---

file should reside on that disk. If you boot from a hard disk, the config.sys should be located in the root directory. If you do not currently have a config.sys, you must create one as follows:

From your DOS prompt, type the following:

```
copy con:config.sys
files=30
buffers=22
```

Now press the F6 key (shorthand for **CTRL-Z**). Press **<ENTER>** and the system will display the message:

```
1 file copied
```

You have just created a config.sys file.

If you already have a config.sys file, check it to ensure that the files and buffers are set to the above minimums. If not, edit the file to add or change the files and buffer commands with the DOS editor, "Edlin" (see your DOS manual), or any other ASCII editor. You must reboot (restart your computer) for the new config.sys to be effective.

Note: As stated in the introduction, your computer must have at least 430K of RAM to use dBXL and the programs in this book.

Path

The path command allows you to run dBXL from directories other than the one in which the dBXL program files are located. This is important if you are running on a hard disk-based system that uses directories to separate programs. For instance, let's say that your dBXL program files are located in a directory called dBXL, and that you also have a directory called AD-DRESS, in which you have placed the files from the Address Book Program. If the path command includes c:\dbxl, and ADDRESS is the current directory, when you type dBXL, DOS will look in the dBXL directory to find the dBXL programs. In other words, the path command tells DOS, "If you can't find the file you're looking for in the current directory, look in the directory (or directories) listed in the path command."

What's the advantage of starting dBXL from ADDRESS or some other directory? If you execute dBXL from ADDRESS, then dBXL will recognize the Address Book Program files without being instructed to change directories. This saves you time, and allows you to run many different programs easily without stopping each time to reset dBXL for the files you are using. Directories listed in the path command are preceded by the drive letter, as in

```
path=c:\dbxl
```

(**NOTE**: If you want to include other directories in the path, such as those for your word processor, communications program, or spreadsheet, separate them with a semi-colon, as in

```
Path=c:\dbxl;c:\wp;c:\xtalk;c:\123
```

The path command should be placed in your autoexec.bat file, so that it is immediately executed when you boot your system. If you do not already have an autoexec.bat file, here's how to create one that incorporates the dBXL path (for a hard disk that functions as the C drive):

```
cd \ <ENTER>
Copy con: autoexec.bat <ENTER>
(name of clock file initialization software, if relevant, then <ENTER>
Date <ENTER> (only if you don't have a built-in clock
function)
Time <ENTER> (only if you don't have a built-in clock function)
path=c:\dbxl <ENTER>
```

To complete the autoexec.bat file, press the **F6** function key (which places a ^Z on the screen). Now press **<ENTER>** and the screen will display:

```
1 file copied
```

This indicates that the batch file was created.

If you already have an autoexec.bat file, edit it with the DOS text editor, "Edlin" (see your DOS manual), or any other ASCII editor, to include the path command. The next time you boot your system, it will know to look in the dBXL directory when it can't find the dBXL startup program in the current directory.

Installation: Hard Disk

There are three different ways for you to install dBXL To Go on your hard disk.

1. The programs can be installed individually, with each program running completely independent of the others in its own directory.

2. Several programs can be installed, each in their own directories, but sharing the utility programs in a common directory.

3. All the programs in the system can be installed and accessed through a master menu program.

The INSTALL.BAT program on the dBXL To Go original diskette will help you copy the files from a compressed file on the original diskette to appropriately named directories on your hard disk for each of these possible installations.

Single Program Option

We will pretend that you want to install the Address Book program in its own directory. First, create a directory on your hard disk to hold the program and data files. Type the DOS command line

```
md \address <ENTER>
```

to create a directory called address under the Root directory. Make this the current, or default, directory by typing:

```
cd \address <ENTER>
```

Then place your dBXL To Go distribution diskette in floppy drive A: and call the dBXL To Go INSTALL.BAT program by typing:

```
a:install s addr <ENTER>
```

The INSTALL program will decompress the utility programs and copy them into the default directory ADDRESS on your hard disk. It will then decompress and copy the program and data files for the Address Book program into the same directory. The program can then be started by typing:

```
dbxl address <ENTER>
```

Don't forget, you will always need to have made ADDRESS (or whatever you have named the new directory) the current DOS directory (using the **cd** command) before entering this command line, in order for dBXL to be able to find all the files necessary to run the Address Book program.

Selected Programs Option

When you want to use more than one of the dBXL To Go programs, the best way to install them is to have each program and its associated data files in one directory, and all the utility programs that they use in common in a separate directory that dBXL knows about. The INSTALL.BAT program will create the directories for you, all you have to do is use the cd command to make the directory you want to be the parent directory current. For example, for ease of access you might want all your dBXL To Go programs to reside in sub-directories just under the "root" directory. First, make sure that the "root" directory is the current directory by typing:

```
cd \ <ENTER>
```

Say that you only want the Time Billing and Invoicing programs installed. With the dBXL To Go original diskette inserted in your floppy drive A:, type:

```
a:install ss time inv <ENTER>
```

The INSTALL.BAT program will proceed to create three sub-directories, \TGTIME, \TGINV, and \TGUTILS; and then decompress and copy the appropriate files into each sub-directory.

The INSTALL.BAT program only recognizes the following abbreviated codes for each of the dBXL To Go programs.

Table of Abreviated Program Codes

Program	Program Prefix
Address Book	ADDR
Invoice	INV
Dynamic Inventory Management	WARE
Note Card	NOTE
Mailing List	MAIL
Time Billing	TIME
Travel Expense Management	TRAV
Sales Lead Management	LEAD
Bibliography	BIBL
Capital Assets Tracking	CAP

If you forget the codes you need, and don't have the book handy when you want to install dBXL To Go, just type

```
a:install <ENTER>
```

without any arguments. INSTALL.BAT will display a help screen showing the codes and options it can recognize.

Master Menu Option

When you select this option, INSTALL.BAT takes care of almost everything for you. Just make sure that you have at least 700,000 bytes of storage free on your hard disk. To do this, type

```
dir <ENTER>
```

and check the 'space available' amount printed at the end of the directory listing. If you have 700,000 or more bytes free, you have enough room for the entire dBXL To Go system on your drive. Make sure that the dBXL To Go original diskette is in floppy drive A:, then type:

```
a:install sm <ENTER>
```

That's all you have to do! INSTALL.BAT creates a directory called \TOGO, copies the program file MAINMENU.PRG into it, then creates 11 sub-directories under \TOGO: one for each program, and a utilities directory for their common utility programs. Once the program has finished decompressing and copying all the programs into their appropriate directories, you can begin running dBXL To Go by typing:

```
dbxl mainmenu <ENTER>
```

The master menu will allow you to select any one of the ten programs in the dBXL To Go system. When you are through working in one program, exiting that program returns you to the master menu, where you can select one of the other dBXL To Go programs or return to the DOS prompt.

Installation: Dual Floppy Systems

The only practical setup for dBXL To Go on a computer with only floppy drives is to allot one floppy diskette for each dBXL To Go program that you wish to run. INSTALL.BAT can be used to install each program on its own diskette by using the **Single Program** option as described above for Hard Disk systems. Instead of creating a directory on the hard disk and making it current, place the dBXL To Go original diskette in the A drive and the blank, formatted floppy disk that you want to hold the dBXL To Go program in the B drive. Make the B drive the currently selected drive by typing

b: **<ENTER>**

and then type

a:install s (program code) **<ENTER>**

INSTALL.BAT will decompress and copy the files needed and copy them onto the new diskette in the B drive. Assuming that you have installed dBXL for a dual-floppy system, you can now place your dBXL work diskette in drive A and type the following sequence of command lines to run the program on the B drive:

```
a: <ENTER>          (Makes A the current drive)
dbxl <ENTER>        (Load and run dBXL)
set default to b:   (Switch back to the B drive)
do ...              (Run the dBXL To Go program that you just
                     installed)
```

Both the program and the data files for the dBXL To Go program will remain on the B diskette. It is a good idea to backup your data by copying the entire diskette periodically with the DOS command DISKCOPY, or some other DOS copy utility, to keep as a backup of your data. You will also probably have to check the diskette regularly to see that you have plenty of space left for new data; if you run out of space on the diskette while you are adding records to the data files or updating indexes to the data files, the program will lock up and YOU WILL PROBABLY LOSE DATA! Check the space available on the diskette by using either the DOS CHKDSK or DIR commands BEFORE you use the program to add data in order to avoid this dismal situation.

Setup

The first time you use any dBXL To Go program, customize it for your system, select screen and report headers, and choose whether you want password protection. The basic setup options offered in all dBXL To Go programs are described in this section. Several of the programs (Invoice, Time Billing, and Capital Assets) also have special setup options, which are discussed in their respective chapters.

To start dBXL To Go program, use the following steps. (Again, the Address Book program is used for the sake of illustration. Substitute the appropriate directory and file name for the program you are using.)

Hard Disk

1. Make ADDRESS the current directory as discussed above, in Installation: Hard Disk, or execute the batch file.

2. If you are not using a batch file, type:

   ```
   dbxl address <ENTER>
   ```

   This will execute dBXL and the Address Book Program, assuming that you have included dBXL in the path of your autoexec.bat file, as described above. Regardless of how you execute the Address Book Program, you will first see the dBXL copyright and license notice. Press **<ENTER>** and the screen will display the message "Creating indexes, please wait". This process may require a few seconds, but it only occurs the first time you run the program after installation. The screen will then be displayed. Press **<ENTER>** and the Main Menu will be displayed.

Basic Setup Options

Once the Main Menu is displayed, select the Utilities option, and the Utilities Menu will be displayed. Select "System Setup," and the following basic options will be displayed on an input screen:

Company/user name. This field places the company's or the user's name on each screen of the program, and on all reports. You may enter a maximum of 40 characters. This field will be automatically centered, so enter your name without leading spaces.

Compress print command. Enter the setup string that changes your dot matrix print to condense print, or that allows you to use a 15-character-per-inch (cpi) or smaller thimble or wheel with your impact printer. The program defaults to 015, which is used as the code for condensed print by IBM, Epson, and many other printer manufacturers. If in doubt, check your printer's manual. If you have a wide carriage printer (132 columns), enter a blank rather than a code. This will ensure that reports are output at the full size.

Note that all setup codes must be entered in three digit sets, separated by a space (e.g., 027 031). Also, the compress print command allows for a maximum of 250 characters, even though the field appears to be only 20 characters. The field will automatically scroll to permit additional characters. Unless you have a laser printer (see Appendix B), it is unlikely that you will input more than four sets of characters (plus a space between each set). If you do exceed 20 characters, your next entry will scroll to the left. To review characters that have scrolled off the screen use the left cursor arrow and the characters will scroll to the right. Press **<ENTER>** when you are done.

Normal print command. Enter the setup string that restores your printer to 10 cpi. This print size is used in summary reports. The program defaults to code 018, the IBM/Epson standard for 10 cpi. The same field and scrolling characteristics described for the condensed print option apply to the normal print command.

Color monitor (Y/N). Select **N** for monochrome monitors. If you have a color monitor, text will appear in yellow, the background will be blue, and reverse video will appear in light blues. Note: If you have a Compaq, use the color setting only if you have an external color monitor. If you use the color setting in monochrome graphics mode, the background will overshadow the individual fields.

Password protection (Y/N). If you choose **N**, the program will always begin with the Main Menu, bypassing the password security module. If you select **Y**, the next time you run the program, you will be prompted to enter a master password (see Utilities 1 and 2 for a greater discussion of the password utility).

Once you enter a master password, the program will ask you to re-enter it for verification (first time only). The program may pause for a few seconds while it processes the password. The Master Password Maintenance Menu will then appear on the screen with options for assigning passwords to others, editing or deleting previously assigned passwords, and displaying current password codes. Hint: If you use the master password to gain access to the program, you will always be presented with the Master Password Maintenance Menu, and will have to exit in order to call up the Main Menu. A shortcut is to assign yourself a regular password for routine use, and only enter the master password when you need to make password changes.

If you or any other user fails to enter a correct password, the system will allow you to try two more times. Note: It is normal for the password program to pause for several seconds (depending on the computer you are using) before allowing you to try again. If you still have not entered the correct password, the program will return to DOS. Since the password security program is virtually indecipherable, we strongly urge you to write down the master password and keep it in a safe place. You may switch password protection off even after you have been using the program. You can also switch it back on at a later date; the codes will remain in the file. (As mentioned above, the Invoice, Time Billing, and Capital Assets programs have additional options; see the Installation and Setup sections in their individual chapters.)

Saving Your Setup Choices

After you press <ENTER> in the last field of the Setup screen, the program will automatically save all the setup information you have entered and return to the Main Menu. If you wish to change any of the setup options at a later date, repeat the above procedure. The easiest way to edit a setup option field is simply to overwrite it. To accept an existing entry, press <ENTER>. When the cursor is in the last field, pressing <ENTER> will save the new setup data. (Note: You can press **CTRL-END** to save your changes at any point in the setup process. **CTRL-END** is a shortcut for pressing <ENTER> in the last field.) Once the Main Menu has been redisplayed, you can begin entering data as described in each program's chapter.

2 Address Book Program

Features

- Menu driven.
- Password protection.
- Comprehensive electronic address book, designed for business or personal use.
- Coding system for tagging and retrieving specific records.
- Prints out large and small Rolodex-type cards, mailing labels, detailed lists, and summary lists.
- Create custom lists with user-specified sort/selection features.

Contents

Introduction

The Address Book Program enables you to create records for all your business and personal contacts. Each record includes an individual's name, title, department, business and home addresses, and business and home telephone numbers. You can also enter a brief comment for each record, and as many as four selection codes. The codes can be used to designate the person's profession, degrees, status, or any other categories of your choice.

Once records are input, you can print out custom lists in several formats; large and small Rolodex-type cards; mailing labels; and standard 8.5 x 11- inch reports. The standard paper report allows you to print either a detailed list or a telephone (summary) list. The telephone list can be extremely valuable when you are traveling, as it contains key information in compact form.

All functions of the Address Book Program are accessed by menus that include instructions on the bottom of the screen. These menus allow you to customize the Address report header and printer specifications, establish passwords, scan records, print reports, and continually update the address list using various file utilities and edit functions.

Before using the program, read through this manual and familiarize yourself with all the input, report, and utilities functions. You may want to set up a practice address book, using two or three addresses to review the functions for the program. Also, create a backup disk for your database file (Address. dbf.). There's no need to back up your program (.prg), format (.fmt), or report (.frm) file. You can always recopy them from your working diskette. You don't have to back up your index files either, since your program creates them if they aren't found in the directory.

At a minimum, back up your .dbf file each time you add or edit records; the few minutes this procedure requires will more than offset the time you would spend if the entire database had to be re-created. Remember, *no* hardware system is infallible; it's better to be safe than sorry!

Finally, if you are an experienced dBXL user and wish to modify the program, refer to the Technical Appendix charts and tables. You will find a program tree that lists the calling program hierarchy, a table that describes each index file, and a list of files required to run the program.

Data Entry Keys

After you have input data, use the Backspace key to erase your entry if you wish to change it, provided that you haven't pressed **<ENTER>**. Alternately, use the cursor and Delete/Insert keys to modify your entry. When you do press **<ENTER>** the cursor will move to the next data input field. If you need to return to a previous entry, use the up cursor key to move the cursor to the field. Enter your changes and press **<ENTER>**, to move on through the input screen. Note that any errors made during data entry can also be corrected later by means of the Edit option (see below).

Installing And Setting Up The Program

Before you begin using the Address Book Program, you will have to install it and set it up. General instructions for installation and setup are in Chapter 1.

Starting The Program

The easiest way to start the Address Book program is to create a batch file. You can also start the program manually by typing

```
do address
```

after starting dBXL (See Chapter 1 startup techniques.)

Regardless of how you begin the Address Program, you will first see the dBXL copyright and license notice. The screen will then display the message "Creating indexes, please wait." This process may require a few seconds, but only occurs the first time you run the program after installation. The Address Book Program Main Menu will then appear.

Creating An Address Book Record

All data is entered into the program through the address input screen, which is called up by selecting Option #1, Add Records from the Main Menu. The Address Input Screen consists of four sections.

1. Identification section. Contains the addressee's name and company.

2. Code/comment section. User-defined code fields and comment fields.

3. Business location section. Contains business address and telephone information.

4. Home location section. Contains the addressee's home address and telephone.

Identification Section

When you select Add Records from the Main Menu, the cursor will move through the following sequence of fields each time you press **<ENTER>**:

1. Name: The Name field actually consists of three separate fields:
    a. Personal title: Enter Mr., Mrs., Dr., or the personal title of your choice.
    b. First name.
    c. Last Name.

2. Title.

3. Department.

4. Company.

Code Comment Section

Code. Space is provided for four codes with three spaces per code. These can be extremely useful for generating custom lists. For instance, if you want to create a top priority contact list, you might enter VIP in one of the code fields. Later, you can ask the program to generate a list of all VIPs in the database. The code field can also identify a person's specialty. Dr. Smith, for example, might have the code RES, for researcher, and a second code, MB, for molecular biologist. The applications of the code fields are limited only by your imagination.

You may structure the codes any way you like, as long as you are consistent. If you code some molecular biologists as MB and others as MOL or BIO, you will have difficulty locating them for editing, and they will not be grouped together on certain reports. We strongly recommend that you keep a list of codes by your computer, to ensure that you or anyone else who inputs data into the Address Book Program will use the correct codes.

Comment. This field can be used to enter remarks, or to list a second telephone number. The comment field appears on the large address card printout (see Generating Reports, below).

Business Location Section

The cursor will move through the following sequence of fields each time you press **<ENTER>**:

1. Address
2. City
3. State
4. Zip
5. Country
6. Telephone

Home Location Section

All fields are identical to the business location section, as is the cursor sequence.

Adding Another Address Book Record

When you press **<ENTER>** while the cursor is in the last field of the Home Location Section, or press **CTRL-END** at any time during data input, the record will be included in the database. A prompt at the bottom of the screen will then ask if you want to add another record. To accept the default **Y** and continue adding records, press **<ENTER>**. If you enter **N**, the program will return to the Main Menu. A record is considered completed when you have supplied a last name. Records input without a last name will not be added to the database.

Note: The space provided for personal title, first name, and last name exceeds the physical dimension of some labels and address file cards. The maximum combined length for the title and names for the Rolodex-type address cards is 32 characters, and 40 characters for the mailing labels. The oversized name files are provided to give you maximum flexibility for input. If your address has a long last name, you might have to abbreviate the first name or use initials; otherwise, the last name will be truncated during output.

Editing/Viewing/Deleting Records

The Scan Function

To recall previously created address book records, select Edit/Delete Records from the Main Menu (Option #2), and choose a criteria by which you will scan for records in the database.

Scanning is used to search for a record or group of records, and display them on the screen. It is useful for two purposes. First, it enables you to pinpoint a specific record for viewing, editing, or deleting, as explained below. Second, you can locate a group of records and display them one by one for editing or deletion.

One way to think of the scan function is to imagine the records on a track. When you scan for everyone in the ABC Company, the program will find the first record that has ABC in the Company field. It will then display that record in scanning format (see below). You can view the rest of the records one after another, forward and backward by pressing **F** and **B**—see editing options, below). The records will appear alphabetically in the order determined by the criteria you selected. If you enter a blank scan criteria and press **<ENTER>** or **ESC**, the program will display the first record in the database, according to the criteria you selected.

Scanning Procedures

The following process is identical for each scan option:

1. Select the criteria field on which you want to scan for records. The Scanning Criteria Input screen will then be displayed. Enter the appropriate information. You can use abbreviations of the name you are seeking; the program will find the first record matching the abbreviations. For example, if you only enter C for scan by name, the program will display the first record starting with the letter C.

2. If any address book records match the word(s) or abbreviation(s) you entered, the record you are seeking will be displayed in Scanning Screen format. You can then use the options described below to edit, view, or delete the information. If there is more than one record for the name or word you entered, the program will display the first one entered. If you entered an abbreviation or contraction of the actual field, the order will be based on the entire field. For example, if you scan on West in the name field, and records with Westfall and Westlake both match the criteria, Westfall will appear first, because it precedes Westlake alphabetically.

3. If no records in the database match the name or word entered in the Scanning Criteria Input screen, the program will display the following message:

```
No records meet your criteria
Press any key to continue
```

Scanning Options

Once you have located the desired address record, you can use any of the functions listed at the bottom of the Scanning screen. These include:

F=Forward, B=Backward. Each time you press **F**, you will browse from one address book record to another. To move backward through the file, press **B**. The program will move backward one record each time the **B** key is pressed. If you try to scan past the end of the file (the record most recently input), or the beginning of the file (the first record entered), the program will beep and remain on the last or first record.

E=Edit. Once you have located an address book record for editing or updating through the Scan option, select item **E**. The system will then enter full screen edit mode, in which each field will be highlighted on the screen as it was during initial data entry. You can move from highlighted field to highlighted field by using the cursor or by pressing**<ENTER>**. Each time you press **<ENTER>**, the cursor will advance one field. Make your changes in a field by using the backspace, insert, or delete keys. The editing process is ended by pressing **CTRL-END** in any field, or pressing **<ENTER>** in the last field of the Home Location Section. Either action will save the information to disk. You can exit without saving the changes to disk by pressing the **ESC** key.

D=Delete. Deletion with the Address Book Program is a two-step process. First, press **D** to mark the record for deletion. MARKED FOR DELETION will then appear above the menu options. Although a record is marked for deletion, it is not actually deleted until you use the Pack function, which is accessed from the Utilities Menu (see below). Records may remain in the marked state indefinitely. Even when you exit the program and return at a later date, records slated for deletion will still be marked.

U=Undelete. If you decide that you don't want to delete a record and haven't used the Pack function yet, you can unmark the record for deletion by selecting the U option. The MARKED FOR DELETION message will then be removed from your screen.

0=Exit. When you select the zero option, the program will return to the Main Menu.

Generating Reports

The Address Book Program uses several report formats and organizational schemes for printing address records. To create any of the reports, select Generate Reports Option #3 from the Main Menu. The Print Menu will then be displayed, offering you two options:

1. Print Entire Database

2. Print Selected Records

Print Entire Database

If you choose Print Entire Database (option #1), the Report Selection Menu will be displayed with following options:

Telephone list . Contains the Name fields (first and last) and Business and Home Telephone numbers. This report is printed on standard 8.5 x 11 inch paper.

Detailed report. Prints all information from each record in compressed type, on standard 8.5 x 11-inch paper.

Mailing labels. Prints the Name fields (first and last), Title, Department, Company, Address, City, State, and Zip on 3.5 x 15/16-inch labels. Note: When you select the Mailing Label option, you will be asked whether you want to use the home or business address.

Large Rolodex-type Cards. Prints out the Name fields (first and last) Business Telephone, Title, Company, Address, City, State, Zip, Home Telephone, Address, and Comment on 3x5-inch cards.

Small Rolodex-type Cards. Prints out the Name fields and Home Business Address/Telephone data on 2x4-inch cards. When you select the small card option, you will be asked whether you want to print business or home data.

Once you have selected the type of report you want to print, a Message Screen will prompt you to:

```
Align printer and press return to continue
```

Make sure your printer is on-line before pressing **<ENTER>**. Otherwise you will get an error message. Retry with your printer on-line.

Print Selected Records

This option from the Print Menu allows you to select specific kinds of records to be printed. Take the following steps:

1. When you press **2**, a Report Criteria Input screen will be displayed. Notice that the criteria screen is identical to the input screens you used to input and edit records, with the exception that only certain fields are highlighted. You can select the records you want to filter from the database by indicating your criteria in the highlighted fields. For example, code VIP will print all records with VIP in the Code field. If you want to further refine the list you can enter additional codes. Note that any field left blank will *not* be included in the filter.

   One caveat: To pass through the filter, a record must meet *all* your search criteria. So if you make the selection filter too fine by adding too many criteria, you will probably not print any records at all. Unfortunately, there is no absolute number of criteria above which the filter function defeats itself; each database has its own limits. With a little experimenting, you can determine the maximum productive levels of criteria to be used for your data.

Once you have entered the criteria by which you wish to filter the database, press **CTRL-END** or **<ENTER>** in the highlighted field. The program will then begin searching for records that match your criteria and create a report from them.

2. If any records match your criteria, the program will display the Criteria Search Results screen, which indicates how many records met your criteria. The Criteria Search Results Screen gives you the following options, in addition to pressing **ESC** to return to the Main Menu.

    ***Press* P *to Print*.** Use this option if you wish to print the selected records. You will be presented with the Report Selection Menu discussed above. The menu will indicate how many records are to be printed, along with the criteria you used to select them. The report formats are the same as those used to print the entire database (see above). Note that when reports are printed after a criteria search, the criteria used will be indicated at the top of the page.

    ***Press* S *to display on screen*.** Before you print a report, you may want to view the address records first to make sure you have retrieved the correct one(s). Or, you may just wish to review the selected records on the screen. This option allows you to do either. When you press **S**, the program will display the first address record that met your search criteria, in Scanning Screen format. If more than one record was found, you can page forward and backward through the selected records by using **F** (forward) and **B** (backward). The principle is the same as that used in the editing process described above.

    After you are finished examining the selected records, press zero to return to the Report Selection Menu. You can then print the selected records, or return to the Main Menu by pressing **0**.

3. If no records are located, the program displays the message:

    ```
    No records meet your criteria
    Press any key to continue
    ```

    The program will then return to the print menu.

Using Utilities

The Address Book Program includes three housekeeping functions. These are accessed from the Utilities Menu, which you used earlier to set up the program. The Utilities Menu is accessed by selecting Option #4 from the Main Menu. The utility options are described below.

Reindex. Occasionally, you may find that the search routines are not operating correctly. The most probable cause for this is a damaged index, which usually results from illegally exiting the program (see Exiting, below, for the proper exit routine). If this should occur, you must reindex the files by selecting Option #1 from the Utilities Menu. The reindexing option will take a variable period of time, depending on the number of records in the file.

Pack invoices. Packing is the final stage used to delete marked records (see Editing/Viewing/Deleting Records, above). Unlike marking a record, though, packing is an irreversible action; once an address record is packed, it no longer exists. After selecting the pack option, the program will display how many records will be packed, and you will be asked to confirm your choice with a **Y** plus an **<ENTER>**. The packing process can take several minutes or longer, since it must update all indexes.

System setup. The Address Book Program uses the dBXL to Go basic setup options. These are described in Chapter 1.

Note: If you want to delete all records and start with a clean database, you can either recopy the .dbf files from your distribution diskette or use the dBXL Zap command to erase all records. Zap simultaneously deletes and packs all records in your database. To use Zap, make the directory in which you keep your Address Book Program files current. Start dBXL, and, at the dBXL prompt, type:

```
use address
```

Next, type:

```
zap
```

dBXL will ask you to confirm the action with a **Y** or **N**. When you select **Y**, all records will be erased and deleted from your database. After zapping, you must reindex to ensure that your indexes correspond to the program.

> **CAUTION**: Zap is an irrevocable command. Therefore, backup your data before zapping it!

Exiting

It is vitally important that you properly exit from the Address Book Program. Failure to do so may cause file or index damage. While it is often possible to remedy the situation by reindexing, the damage may be permanent, in which case you must start over again by copying the files from your diskette and re-entering your data, or restoring your database from your most recent back-up copy. Given the needless waste of time and the aggravation in reconstructing a database, *always exit by pressing* **0** in the menu you are working with until you reach the Main Menu. Pressing **0** at the Main Menu will close all database files and return you to a Sign-Off screen that asks you if you wish to leave the program. Entering **Y** returns you to DOS. Entering **N** returns you to the Main Menu. Note: If you are running an uncompiled program, pressing **X** will return you to the XL dot prompt.

3 Manual For Invoice Program

Features

- Menu driven.
- Password protection.
- Comprehensive input screen automatically computes extended price, sales tax, and gross profit.
- Generates invoices, client statements, and delinquency notices.
- Automatically numbers invoices.
- Creates custom invoice letterhead.
- Tracks invoices by age, customer, or client.
- Produces invoice master listing, sales representative report, productivity report, sales tax report, and accounts receivable report.

Contents

Introduction

This program enables you to create invoices, track them through the billing cycle, generate demand notices, and create reports indicating the status of your accounts receivable. While it is not designed to replace your entire accounting system, it can be effectively used in both retail and service businesses. The invoice input form includes entry spaces for unit price and quantity, which can also be used for time spent and hourly rate. (If you need a finer gradation of time spent and hourly rates, see the Time Billing Program, Chapter 7.)

The Invoice Program is extremely flexible and easy to use. Entering invoices is facilitated by the program's auto-entry and calculation features. Once you have filled out an invoice for a customer or client, it will only be necessary to enter the first and last name, and the program will look up and fill in demographic, tax, and other constant information. The program also calculates extended prices as you enter units and unit price. It then automatically computes and adds the tax, giving you subtotals and totals for the invoice. If you enter the cost of the goods or service, the profit analysis feature shows your gross profit and profit margin.

Before using the program, read through this manual and familiarize yourself with all the input, report, and utility functions. You may want to set up a practice invoicing system, using two or three invoices to review the functions of the program. Also, create a backup disk for your database files (invoice.dbf and invarch.dbf).

There's no need to back up your program (.prg), format (.fmt), or report (.frm) files. You can always recopy them from your working diskette. You don't have to back up your index files either, since your program creates them if they aren't found in the directory.

At a minimum, back up your .dbf files each time you add or edit records; the few minutes the procedure requires will more than offset the time you would need to spend if the entire database had to be recreated. Remember, *no* hardware system is infallible, and it's better to be safe than sorry!

Finally, if you are an experienced dBXL user and wish to modify the program, refer to the Technical Appendix charts and tables. You will find a program tree that lists the calling program hierarchy, a table that describes each index file, and a list of files required to run the program.

Data Entry Keys

After you have input data, you may use the Backspace key to erase your entry (provided that you haven't pressed **<ENTER>**). Alternately, you can use the cursor and Delete/Insert keys to modify your entry. When you do press **<ENTER>**, the cursor will move to the next data input field. If you need to return to a previous entry, use the up cursor key to move the cursor to the field. Enter your changes and press **<ENTER>** to move on through the input screen. Note that any errors made during data entry can also be corrected later by means of the Edit option (see below).

Installing And Setting Up The Program

Before you begin using the Invoice Program, you will have to install it and set it up. General instructions for installation and setup are contained in Chapter 1. Additional setup options are described in Chapter 12, Utilities.

Starting The Program

The easiest way to start the Invoice Program is to create a batch file. You can also start the program manually by typing

```
do invoice
```

after starting dBXL (see Chapter 1 for specifics of both start-up techniques).

Regardless of how you begin the Invoice Program, you will first see the dBXL copyright and license notice. The screen will display the message "Creating indexes, please wait." This process may require a few seconds, but it only occurs the first time you run the program after installation. The Invoice Program Main Menu will then appear.

Creating Invoices

To call up an Invoice Input Screen, select Option #1, Input Invoices, from the Main Menu. The Invoice Input Screen (also referred to as the Master Invoice Display in this manual) consists of six sections:

1. Status section. Provides basic information about the invoice and its disposition.

2. Demographics section. Contains information about the client name and address.

3. Detail information section. Contains specific information about the order, its tax status, and shipping.

4. Item description/computation section. Gives detailed information about the goods or services sold, and computes totals.

5. Profit analysis section. Computes profit based on invoice total and cost of goods.

6. Messages/prompts section. Displays prompts and options.

Status Section

The following fields are located in the Status section:

Rep. Enter the sales rep's name or ID number. You can input up to eight alphabetic or numeric characters. The key, as with all database information, is to be *consistent*; Smith,P. (with no space after the comma) will be treated differently than Smith, P. (with a space after the comma). Any inconsistencies will produce inaccurate reports.

Invoice. When you first call up a blank invoice input screen, the system automatically assigns a number beginning with 000001. If you want to change the starting number, you may do so when you have finished entering all data into the input form. At that point, the program will ask you if you want to edit any information. You may for example, want your invoice sequence to begin with the last two digits or last digit of the year (e.g., if 100001 or 870001 were the first invoices, the next would be 100002 or 870002, respectively). A word of caution: If you do edit subsequent invoice numbers, be careful not to duplicate existing numbers.

Nonlabeled fields. In addition to automatically inserting the invoice number in the Status Area, the program also inserts the system date (which is why it is very important to type in the correct date when you start the computer), and indicates that the invoice status is OPEN (unpaid).

Note: At most points during data entry, you may go back to a previous entry in the current section by using the left arrow. You can also advance forward by pressing **<ENTER>** successively; each time you press **<ENTER>**, you will advance one field. Due to the logic of the validation and calculation features of the invoice input program, you generally cannot back up to a previous section during the input process. You can, of course, correct any errors after input by means of the edit option (see below).

Demographics Section

Once you have finished entering the Rep field in Section 1, you will see two highlighted fields after the word Bill. These are for the client's or customer's first and last name, in that order. The cursor will be at the left-hand edge of the first field. Enter the appropriate first and last name. Note: You *must* have an entry in the last name field; otherwise, you will not be able to edit invoices.

If this is the first invoice for a particular client or customer, five more highlighted fields will appear on the screen, after you enter information in the last name field and press **<ENTER>** underneath the two fields you have just filled in. If you have previously billed this client, the auto entry feature will be activated (see below). The line immediately under the first and last name fields is for the client or customer's company. If relevant, enter the company name. If not, press return and leave the line blank. *Do not begin entering the address on the second line*. Enter the address on the third line, and the city, state, and zip in their respective fields on the fourth line.

Once you have filled in the name, company, and address, the words Ship To will appear on the right side of the screen, with highlighted fields for the first name. If the Ship To address is the same as the Bill To address, leave the first name field blank and press <ENTER>; the program will automatically repeat all the information from the Bill To section in the Ship To section. If the Ship To address is different from the Bill To address, enter the Ship To first name and press return. The program will display blank highlighted fields for the last name, company, address, city, state, and zip for you to fill in.

Auto entry feature. Once you have entered a client or customer into the database, the program will automatically look up the demographic information. (It does this by searching for a match with the first three letters of the first and last name.) If you enter Paul Smith in the Ship To section, and Paul Smith has already been entered, the program will fill in all other Bill To information, Ship To information, and the Detail Information in Section 3. If the information the program enters is correct, keep pressing <ENTER> until you reach Section 4, Item/Description. If you wish to change any field, simply overwrite the existing information, and proceed to Section 4.

Detail Information Section

This section provides spaces to enter the following information:

Tele. Enter the Customer's telephone number.

P.O. Enter the purchase order number, if relevant.

Tax. If you enter YES (the default) in the tax field, the program will automatically compute the sales tax on the invoice based on the tax rate you entered during the setup phase (see Utilities). If you enter anything other than YES in the tax field, the program will *not* compute the tax. Note: You might use this field to indicate that the client or customer is tax exempt, in which case you can enter a Tax Exemption number. You can also use it as a memo for tax exemption (e.g., out-of-state).

Terms. Use this as a reminder (e.g., net 10, COD, etc).

C.C. If relevant, enter the credit card name, number, and expiration date.

Ship. Enter the shipping method (e.g., UPS ground, Fed X, etc). This is a text field and does not affect the shipping charge computation. Once you have filled out the Detail Information, you are ready to list the goods or services sold to the customer.

Item Description/Computation Section

When you begin to enter data in Section 4, three highlighted fields appear next to each other, constituting the first item listing. The first field is for the quantity, the second is for the description, the third is for the unit price. Note: For consulting work, you might use quantity for the number of hours, and unit price for the hourly rate. If you are working on a fixed-fee basis, enter 1 for quantity and the fixed fee for the unit price. In any case, you *must* enter a value in the quantity field for the invoice to total.

Once you have entered the unit price and pressed <**ENTER**>, the program will automatically calculate the extended price, and the cursor will move to the next line item, which will also have three fields highlighted for quantity, description, and unit price. Up to six lines of items can be entered.

To indicate that you have input your last item, enter blanks for an entire line (quantity, description, and unit price). The program will subtotal the items, compute and add the tax (if you indicated YES for the tax field in Section 3), and ask you to enter the shipping charges. It will then calculate a grand total. After the total is complete, the cursor will be at the left edge of the highlighted field call Deposit. Enter any down payments or deposits that have been made, and the balance due will be adjusted. Deposits must be negative numbers. If you enter a positive number, it will automatically be converted to a negative one.

Note: Since the invoice program will not print any line with a zero or blank quantity, you can insert private comments on your screen by entering a quantity of zero and then typing a comment in the description field. For example, you might want to reference the kind of work you performed or the source of goods sold. Such comments will not print on the invoice. Alternatively, if you want the comment to appear, enter a quantity of 1 and a price of 0. This will not affect the total.

Profit Analysis Section

After pressing <**ENTER**> in the Deposit field of Section 4, the cursor will go to the highlighted field underneath Cost in section five. If you know the cost of the goods or services you are invoicing, enter it in this field. The program will then compute your profit and its percentage of the total invoice. If you do not wish to compute the profit at this time, simply enter a blank.

Messages/Prompts Section

When you press <**ENTER**> in the Cost field, you indicate that all information has been input into the invoice form. The program will then ask

```
Do you want to save input (Y/N)?
```

If correct, enter **Y** and the invoice will be added into the database, and you will be presented with a completed invoice together with the full edit/update/scan/print option menu. (See below for a complete discussion of the editing options.) If you are finished with this invoice, press **ESC** or **0** (zero) to exit. You will then be asked:

```
Do you want to enter another invoice (Y/N)?
```

If you enter **Y**, you will be presented with another blank invoice form. If you enter **N**, the program will return to the main menu.

Editing/Viewing Invoices

The Main Menu offers you two choices for editing invoices that you have previously created: Scan Invoices (Option #2) and Find Invoices (Option #3)

Scan Invoices

Scanning is an extremely fast method of locating an invoice. To use it, however, you must know the customer's or client's last name or the invoice number. When you select this option from the Main Menu, you will be asked whether you want to scan by Last Name or Invoice #, and you'll be given a highlighted field in a submenu to enter your selection. You must enter the exact last name or abbreviation of the last name, or the invoice number for the scan to locate the desired record. If no records in the database match the last name or invoice number you entered, the program will again prompt you to enter a last name or invoice number.

Assuming that you have correctly entered the desired last name or invoice number, the invoice you are seeking will be displayed in Scanning Screen format . If there is more than one invoice for the last name you entered, the program will display the most recent one. You can browse through the other invoices by pressing **B** to go backward and **F** to go forward through the list. (See Master Invoice Options, below, for more information on the browse function and various editing/printing functions that can be preformed after locating a record.)

If you enter a blank in response to last name or invoice number and press **<ENTER>** or **ESC**, the program will display the first record in the database. You can then page through the remaining records using the Forward command, described below.

Find Invoices

The Find function allows you to locate information by last name or company name. Unlike the scan option, however, it can search on the whole last name or company name for both the Bill To and Ship To locations, or just the first few letters, and locate matching invoices. The program will then display a list of the invoices that match your input, and ask which one you would like to view in detail. After you input the desired number, the program will display the invoice you selected in the Scanning Screen format and ask if you wish to edit or print it. If no invoices are found, the list will be blank. Pressing **<ENTER>** takes you back to the Main Menu.

As with the Scan Invoice option, you can page backwards using **B** and then forward using **F** until you find the record you are seeking.

Scanning Options

Once you've located an invoice through Scan or Find, Section 5 (Messages/Prompts) of the invoice form will display a number of options.

F=Forward, B=Backward. Whenever you use either Scan by Invoice # or Find, the invoices are displayed by invoice number. By pressing **F** or **B,** you will page forward or backward in the database. Note that Forward means higher invoice numbers. Once you've located the record in question, you can use any of the functions described in this section. If you press **F** when you are at the end of the file—the most recent record—the program will display End of File and will wait for another command. Likewise, if you browse past the first record, the program will display Beginning of File.

Note: If you access the Master Invoice Display via the Name Scan option, the invoices will be sorted alphabetically by name with the most recent invoice for each name displayed first. Forward is then defined as moving to a later dated invoice for a given client or the next higher name alphabetically if there are no more invoices for the current client.

E=Edit. Once you have located a record for editing through Scan Invoice option or Find Invoice option, select item **E**, and the system will enter full screen edit mode. Each field that can be edited (i.e., not calculated by the system) will be highlighted on the screen. You can move from highlighted field to highlighted field by using the cursor keys or by pressing **<ENTER>**. (Each time you press **<ENTER>**, the cursor will advance one field.) Make your changes in a field by using the Backspace, Insert, and Delete keys. The editing process is affirmed or ended by pressing **CTRL-END** in any field, or by pressing **<ENTER>** while on the last entry (Section 5, the Cost field). Either action will save the information to disk. You can exit without saving the changes to disk by pressing the **ESC** key.

U=Update. Update allows you to change four fields: The Status of the invoice (OPEN or PAID), the Shipping Costs, the Deposit, and the Cost (of goods/services). When you select **U**, the program will go into full screen edit *for those fields only.* You may move between the highlighted fields by using the cursors or the **<ENTER>** key. Press **CTRL-END** when you have finished editing and wish to return to the main menu.

$=Paid. This function is a shortcut that allows you to change the Status from OPEN to PAID without going into full-screen editing.

P=Print Invoice. The print routine for invoices assumes that you will be using standard 8.5 x 11-inch paper stock (see the Reports section for general printing requirements). The Invoice print routine starts printing at the position of the print head when you issue the print command. It uses the Top Spacing that you specified in the setup process to determine how far down the page to start printing. Since it issues a page eject at the end of the print cycle to advance to the same position on the next invoice form, the user must ensure that Top of Form has been set for the starting position. This is required since the print routine suppresses the printing of all blank lines on the invoice and must use the eject command to move to the top of the next form. If you specified a Header Text, the print routine will start printing it one line down from the print head position at the start of printing.

K=Print Packing Slips. Packing slips list the line items and descriptions of an order. They are identical to invoices, except that they do not contain any financial information.

D=Demand Notices. The program generates an all-purpose demand notice for recalcitrant bill payers. (See the discussion on customizing invoice and demand letter text later in this chapter for an explanation of how to change the wording to create a custom demand notice.) Note: You can generate delinquent invoice demand letters in batches from the Reports Menu (see below).

Generating Customer Documents And Reports

If you specified one printer during the setup operation (see Chapter 1), all reports and invoices will be sent to the printer defined as LPT1:. If you specified two printers, reports will be printed on LPT1: and invoices will be printed on LPT2:. If you are going to use two printers, we recommend that you use two parallel printers on two parallel ports set to LPT1: and LPT2:. Other configurations will work, but may be more difficult to correctly set up.

Note: If you terminate a print routine abnormally (i.e., by turning the printer off or by taking the printer off-line in the middle of a print cycle), the program will not have the opportunity to reset the printer address, since the system operates with two printers by redefining the address of the default printer. As a result, it may print to the wrong printer, even at the DOS level after you leave dBXL. In that event, you must reassign the printer by exiting the invoicing program correctly and rebooting the system (press and hold **CTRL** and **ALT** and then press **DEL**). The best solution is to make sure that you are ready to print, and that you have sufficient paper and ribbon before you select the Report or Print option. The following sections describe various types of notices and forms that can be printed.

As with invoices, packing slips, and demand notices, the print routine for reports assumes that 8.5 x 11-inch paper will be used. It differs, though, in that it automatically sets the printer to use compressed print. The program is preset with the command sequence 015, which is the standard for IBM and EPSON printers. If the printer used for reports requires a different command sequence to set it to compressed print, the sequence must be changed during setup (see Chapter 1). Refer to your printer manual to determine what command sequence is required to set it for compressed print. If your printer emulates an IBM or Epson printer, you can use the default setting. All reports print to the printer attached to LPT1: unless otherwise stated.

Once you have selected the type of report you want to print, a Message Screen will prompt you to

```
Align printer and press return to continue
```

Make sure your printer is on-line before pressing **<ENTER>.** Otherwise you will get an error message. Retry with your printer on-line.

Report Menu

The Report Menu is accessed by selecting Option #4 from the Main Menu. The following nine reports are available.

List of all invoices. The list of all invoices prints a single line of information about each invoice, regardless of status, and constitutes your master listing of the database. The headings are: Customer, Company, Date, Invoice #, Product, Invoice Total, and Status.

After selecting *List of all invoices* from the menu, you will be asked to indicate a start and end date. You must enter a valid start and end date. To print all invoices, enter a start date before you input your first invoice, and an end date beyond your last one. Note: The program will not accept an invalid date. Rather, it will persistently ask you for a valid one until you supply it. If you have already begun entering numbers and wish to exit, use the Backspace or Delete key to clean out the field until it is entirely blank, then press the **ESC** key to return to the Report Menu.

Once you've entered the desired dates, the program will ask whether you want to organize the report by Bill-To-Last-Name (**N**) or by Invoice Number (**I**). Finally, you will be asked if you want to print the report (**Y**) on your printer or send it to the screen (**N**). Printing is recommended, since the report requires 132 columns of data and the screen can only display an 80-column contraction of it. Further, the report will quickly scroll of the screen, making it difficult to read. If you do display on the screen you must press **CTRL-NUM LOCK** to pause the scrolling. Press <**ENTER**> to resume.

Upon completion of the reports, you will be asked to press the <**ENTER**> key to continue. This is used to prevent the system from scrolling the end of the report off the screen.

List of open invoices. This report is identical to the *List of all invoices*, except that it only includes those invoices that have not yet been paid (i.e., those with an OPEN status). The procedure for generating it is the same.

List of paid invoices. This is also identical to the *List of all invoices*, but only includes invoices that have a status of PAID. You generate it the same way as you do the above two reports.

List of invoices by amount sequence. This report allows you to print a list of all invoices that fall between the dates and amounts you specify. It is extremely useful for matching up an unidentified check with the correct invoice. For example, let's say you receive a check for $230 dated October 17, 1986, but without any supporting documentation to identify the invoice with which it is associated. You could enter 09/01/86 as the starting date and 10/17/86 as the ending date, and $230 as both the starting and ending dollar amount. The report should indicate the invoice in question. If you had several checks, say $200, $400, and $450, all without documentation, enter the staring dollar as $200 and the ending dollar as $550.

Tax report . This report selects and lists all invoices for the period that have a non-zero sales tax amount, and produces a report that includes Invoice #, Customer, Date, Product, Total,

Taxable Amount, and Tax. As with the first three options above, the tax report requires you to specify the range of dates for reporting. After doing so, you must answer the question, "Do you want to print report (Y/N)?" Entering **Y** sends the report to the printer, **N** creates the report on your screen.

Sales representative performance report. The performance report shows all transactions, OPEN and PAID (or any other status you enter except VOID), for a given period, sorted by sales representative. Further, it sorts the transactions for each sales representative chronologically, so you can track his or her activity through the period. The fields on the performance report are: Sales representative, Invoice #, Customer, Date, Product, Total, Cost, and Profit. The report calculates subtotals for each sales rep and a total for your sales force as a whole.

After accessing this option from the Report Menu, you will be asked to indicate the starting and ending dates for the report, and whether you want it printed (press **Y**). If you answer **N**, the report will be displayed on the screen. If you request printed output, you will be asked whether you want page breaks between the sales representatives.

Delinquency report and second notices. The delinquency report lists all invoices generated before a specified cutoff date, that are still in an OPEN status. The report is sorted by invoice number, and includes Invoice #, Date, Total, Product, Customer, and Telephone number.

After entering the cutoff date, you must indicate whether you want the program to create a double-spaced summary report of all delinquent invoices, or whether you want individual Second Notices for each overdue invoice. The Second Notice uses the same format as the Demand Letter produced from the Master Invoice Display.

Client statement. The client statement is a summary of all open invoices, showing invoice date, invoice number, outstanding balance, interest due on outstanding balances over 30 days, and the current amount due. After selecting this option from the Report Menu, you will be asked to indicate the client's name or the client's company name.

Aged accounts receivable report. This report can be specified by client name or company name. You can also generate a report for all clients and companies by selecting Option #3, ALL, from the submenu. After indicating whether you want a report for specific clients/companies or ALL, you can create a hardcopy report by entering **Y** when asked if you want to print the report. If you want to view the report on the screen, press **N** when prompted.

Using Utilities

The invoicing program includes six housekeeping functions. It also includes the system setup program, which you used the first time you ran the program (see Chapter 1). The housekeeping utilities include:

Delete Invoices. Although the program allows you to delete invoices, in general the practice should be avoided. Much of the program's integrity as an accounting and management tool derives from its ability to maintain a record of all transactions, including those that you might want to delete. At some time in the future you may want to determine what happened to a particular transaction; if you deleted it, the task will be extremely difficult.

A better practice is to set the status to VOID. This will eliminate the record from the critical report, but will leave it in the system should you need to reference it. If you are considering deleting a PAID record for the purpose of efficiency or reducing the size of the database (the smaller the database, the faster the program), you can remove it from the active file by archiving it (see the archiving discussion, below).

If you must delete a record, first locate it through Scan or Find, (see above), and then change its status to DELETE by selecting **E** from the options section and editing the status field. Once that is done, call up the Utility menu from the Main Menu and select the Delete option. You will then be asked to enter the *exact* invoice number you want deleted, and then confirm that it is the record that you wish to delete. The deletion process only marks the record, so it is not considered in any report or calculations. It is therefore possible to recall the invoice (if you remember the invoice number; see Recall invoice option below). To permanently remove the record, you must pack the invoice file after marking the invoice for deletion (see Pack option below).

Note: If you want to delete all records and start with a clean database, you can either recopy the .dbf files from your distribution diskette or use the dBXL Zap command to erase all records. Zap simultaneously deletes and packs all records in your database. To use Zap, make the directory in which you keep your Invoice Program files current. Start dBXL, and then at the dBXL prompt type

```
use invoice
```

Next, type

```
zap
```

dBXL will ask you to confirm the action with a **Y** or **N.** When you select **Y**, all records will be erased and deleted from your database. Repeat this procedure for the archive database, Invarch. After zapping both databases, you must reindex to ensure that your indexes correspond to the program.

> **CAUTION:** Zap is an irrevocable command, and there is no way to recover a zapped file. Therefore, back up your data before zapping it!

Recall invoice. The recall option allows you to retrieve an invoice from limbo and return it to the active file, provided that you have not packed the database. When you select this option you will be asked to indicate which invoice you wish to recall, and to confirm your choice.

Pack invoices. Packing, unlike deleting, is an irreversible action; once an invoice is packed, it no longer exists. After selecting the pack option, you will be asked to confirm your choice. The packing process can take several minutes or longer, since it must update all indexes.

Archive invoices. After continual use, the program will likely require more time to conduct search and update procedures. This is a result of the database expansion; it simply takes longer to search all the records. The solution to this minor problem is to archive old and completed records.

The process for archiving records is to select a cutoff date. All invoice records with an invoice date earlier than the cutoff date and not in the OPEN status will be deleted from the active file and added to the archive file. Note that there is no method for moving data back from the archive to the active file. The archive database can only be accessed via dBXL, or by carefully renaming the archive file to Invoice.dbf and reindexing. Only do this in a separate, temporary directory to avoid overwriting the main Invoice database. Also, be sure your backup is current before beginning this procedure.

It is possible to move data between these files using dBXL, but this is not recommended. Therefore, you should only archive data that you will not have to retrieve. A good rule of thumb is to archive data only after you have closed your books for the period. As a safeguard against including open invoices, the system program will only archive invoices that do not have OPEN as their status.

Reindexing. Occasionally, you may find that the search routines are not operating correctly. The most probable cause for this is a damaged index. This usually results from illegally exiting the program (see below for proper exiting routines). If this should occur, you must reindex the files by selecting Option #5 from the Utility Menu. The reindexing option will take a variable period of time depending on the number of records in the file and the type of computer you are using.

System Setup. The Invoice Program uses all of the basic setup options discussed in Chapter 1. In addition, the Invoice Setup Screen offers the following special options:

1. Number of Printers. The program allows you to run two different printers, one for invoices, the other for statements. If you indicate that you have two printers, the system will automatically output invoices to LPT2:, and statements and reports to LPT1:. If you specify one printer, the program will direct all output to LPT1:.

2. State Sales Tax Rate. For the program to automatically calculate the sales tax on each invoice, you must enter the appropriate rate for your state. Note that the format is decimal, so that five percent would be entered as 0.05, not 5.00.

3. Top Spacing for Invoice. If you choose to print invoices on your own letterhead, you must indicate how far down the page the printing should begin, so that it will not overwrite your name or address. Enter the appropriate number of lines in the space provided. If you wish to create a letterhead using the Header Text option (see Below), you must still indicate where the body of the invoice is to be printed by indicating the desired top spacing. This is especially important if you wish to modify the invoice text you use and the available line of print per page on your printer.

4. Header Text. This option allows you to print a letterhead of your own choosing. You can enter up to five lines, maximum 60 characters each. Type in each line exactly as you wish it to appear on your invoices. You can enter a single- or double-dashed line to separate the header from the body of the invoice. If you enter a header text, you must ensure that the top spacing is set at 7 (lines) or greater. Otherwise, the text will be overwritten by the body of the invoice. Note: This setup option does not automatically center text, as the company/user option does. Position your entries exactly as you would like them to appear in print. When you finish entering your header and press **<ENTER>**, your setup choices will be saved and the Main Menu will be redisplayed.

Exiting

It is vitally important that you properly exit from the Invoice Program. Failure to do so may cause file or index damage. While it is often possible to remedy the situation by reindexing, the damage may be permanent, in which case you must start over again by copying the files from your working diskette and re-entering your data, or restoring your database from your most recent backup copy. Given the needless waste of time and the aggravation in reconstructing a database, *always exit by pressing* **0** *in the menu you are working with until you reach the Main Menu*. Pressing **0** at the Main Menu will close all database files and return you to a Sign-Off screen that asks you if you wish to leave the program. Entering **Y** returns you to DOS, and entering **N** returns you to the Main Menu. Note: If you are running an uncompiled program, pressing **X** will return you to the dBXL prompt.

Customizing Invoice and Demand Letter Text

You can change the wording at the bottom of the invoice, demand letter, or client statement with any word processor capable of editing ASCII text. The program generating the invoice form is call Invlet.prg; the demand letter file is invdmd.prg, and the client statement is found at the bottom of Invrep.prg. These .prg files are all contained in the procedure file Invproc.prg. You can load any of these files into your word processor and change the text, provided that you *do not modify any dBXL code and that each line does not exceed 60 characters*. Be certain to resave the edited programs under the same file name, including the .prg extension. Note: Most word processors default to a different extension than .prg, so you must rename the file accordingly.

4 Manual For Dynamic Inventory Management Program

Features

- Menu driven.
- Password protection.
- Comprehensive system for tracking inventory purchases against customer sales.
- Automatically tracks quantities of goods purchased at various prices, and computes average purchase price.
- Can be set up to operate as LIFO or FIFO system.
- User-specified code for location of inventory items.
- Auto lookup of part types, suppliers, and customers.
- Calculates average cost and profit of product sold.
- Calculates average sales price and profit of products purchased.

Contents

Introduction

The Inventory Management Program is designed to help small businesses keep track of their inventory levels for various product lines. Each time you enter a stock purchase, the database is updated to reflect current inventory levels. When a sale is made, the inventory level is automatically adjusted. The program performs two types of calculations: extended price, if you enter quantity and unit price; or unit price, if you enter quantity and extended price. The program also has an auto-lookup function that facilitates data entry. Each part number, supplier, and customer is assigned a code number. All you have to do is enter the appropriate code number, and the system will recognize the correct item or company.

A unique feature of the Inventory Management Program is its ability to allocate inventory lots according to LIFO (last in, first out) or FIFO (first in, first out) accounting methods. The program also allows you to track inventory from multiple stock-room sites, and to sort reports by location. The following reports are available with the program:

1. *Detail reports.* Provides comprehensive information of inventory purchase and sales records.

2. *Summary reports.* Only provides subtotals for purchase and sales data.

3. *Support file reports.* Prints out contents of files used for auto lookup.

All functions of the Inventory Management Program are accessed by menus that include instructions on the bottom of the screen. These menus allow you to customize the program report header and printer specifications, establish passwords, scan records, print reports, and update the inventory records file using various file utilities and edit functions.

Before using the program, read through this manual and familiarize yourself with all the input, report, and utility functions. You may want to set up a practice inventory system, using two or three inventory records to review the functions of the program. Also, create a backup disk for your database files (warebuy.dbf, wareclnt.dbf, warepart.dbf, waresale.dbf, and ware supl.dbf). There is no need to back up your program (.prg), format (.fmt), or report (.frm) files. You can always recopy them from your working diskette. You don't have to back up your index files either, since your program creates them if they aren't found in the directory.

At a minimum, back up your .dbf files each time you add or edit records; the few minutes that the procedure requires will more than offset the time you would need to spend if the entire database had to be recreated. Remember, *no* hardware system is infallible, and it's better to be safe than sorry!

Finally, if you are an experienced dBXL user and wish to modify the program, refer to the Technical Appendix charts and tables. You will find a program tree that lists the calling program hierarchy, a table that describes each index file, and a list of files required to run the program.

Data Entry Keys

Provided that you haven't pressed **<ENTER>**, you may use the Backspace key to erase your entry, or the cursor arrows and Delete/Insert keys to modify your entry after you have input data. When you do press **<ENTER>**, the cursor will move to the next data input field. Enter your changes and press **<ENTER>** to move through the input screen. Note that any errors made during data entry can also by corrected later by means of the Edit option.

Installing And Setting Up The Program

Before you begin using the Inventory Program, you will have to install it and set it up. General instructions for installation and setup are in Chapter 1.

Starting The Program

The easiest way to start the Inventory Program is to create a batch file. You can also start the program manually by typing

```
do ware
```

after starting dBXL (See Chapter 1 for specifics of both startup techniques).

Regardless of how you begin the Inventory Program, you will first see the dBXL copyright and license notice. The screen will display the message "Creating indexes, please wait." This process may require a few seconds, but it only occurs the first time you run the program after installation. The Inventory Program Main Menu will then appear.

Entering Inventory Records

Data is entered into the program through the Purchase Input screens and the Sales Input screens. Before you can enter data into either input screen, however, you must prepare various support files that contain information about your part numbers, suppliers, and customers. Once you have entered the basic information into the support files, the program will automatically insert it into the appropriate field on each purchase and sales record you create.

For example, if you have indicated in the part-number support file that B1221 corresponds to WIDGET, when you later enter B1221 in the Purchase Input screen the program will automatically insert WIDGET into the part-name field, and show you the current number in stock. Similarly, if you assign 101 as the customer number for SMITH & COMPANY, when you enter 101 in the Sales Input screen, the program will fill in SMITH & COMPANY in the customer field.

To create a support file record, select Option #3 from the Main Menu. The Support File Menu will then be displayed. Use the following steps to fill out the input screens.

Support Files

ADDING A CUSTOMER SUPPORT RECORD

Customer information is used when you enter information into the Sales Input screen. To add a customer support file record, select Option #1 from the Support Menu, and the program will display the Customer Input screen. The screen contains two fields:

Number. Even if you do not use customer numbers, you must assign one in order to use this program. The number can be any combination of six alphabetic or numeric designations such as A-7000.

Name. Input the name of the customer. This will be used on sales records. To save the information into the database, press **<ENTER>** after entering the customer name. You can also save the data at any time, by pressing **CTRL-END**. If you do not want to save your entries, press **ESC**.

ADDING A SUPPLIER SUPPORT RECORD

Select Option #2 from the Support File Menu. An input screen with fields for the supplier's name and number will appear. The entry and saving mechanics are identical to those just described for the customer support record. Note: You must enter a supplier number for the program to function; Up to six alphanumeric characters may be used.

ADDING A PART-NUMBER RECORD

Option #3 of the Support File Menu calls up an input screen with fields for a part number and part description. As with the other support files, you must enter a part number of up to 15 alphanumeric characters. Press **<ENTER>** after entering the part name, or press **CTRL-END** to add the part-number support record to file.

Entering Purchase Transactions

When you select Option #1 from the Main Menu, a blank Purchase Input screen will be displayed. Each time you press **<ENTER>**, the cursor will move through the following sequence of fields:

Stock #. Enter a number or code to identify the purchase. You can enter up to 15 alphanumeric characters. Take some time to plan your system so that the stock number provides the maximum amount of information about the acquisition. Note: You must input a stock number. If you leave the Stock# field blank, the program will terminate the data input process and return to the Main Menu.

Part #. This field must be filled in, or else you will end the data input session when you press ⟨**ENTER**⟩. Enter a valid part number (i.e., one that has been entered into a support file record). If the number is valid, the description of the part will appear in the next field, Description. If there is no support file record with that part number, the bottom of the input screen will display the following message:

```
Part Number Not Found, Press <enter> To Continue
```

At this point, you have two options. Either press **<ENTER>** and enter the correct number, or exit the input screen and create a support file record for the part number you wish to input. To exit the program, overwrite whatever you typed in the Part# field by pressing the space bar. When the field is blank, press **<ENTER>**. The Main Menu will be displayed, after which you can create a support file record.

Description. Filled in by the system (see Part# field, above).

Location. You can use this field to indicate in which stockroom, or in which area of a stockroom, the part is located. Since this field can be used to organize reports, you must be absolutely consistent in the way you input data in this field. Otherwise, similar records will not be grouped together on printouts. For this reason, you are better off using a code than a word. Code 01 is more likely to be input the same way than Central Station, which some operators might conceivably abbreviate as "Central Sta", some as "Central Sta. "(with a period), and still others as just "Central" or "Cent". You could also develop a coding system that would provide a great deal of information. For instance, 01-A could be used to designate a specific area within the Central Station facility. Don't go overboard, though; a coding system that is extremely complex can be just as conducive to input errors as individual words.

Whether you use codes, words, or abbreviations, keep a list of official entries by the computer so that everyone plays by the same data entry rules. If you develop a coding system, make sure that the code list explains the grammar for expanding existing codes.

Comment. Use this field to enter any notations about the part or its acquisition. You can leave it blank if you wish.

P.O.#. Enter the purchase order number related to the acquisition. This is an optional field.

Date. This field is for the date of the acquisition. Enter data as MM/DD/YY. You use it for the date on the purchase order, or the date that the inventory arrived. Whichever you choose, be consistent in your use, since the date is the basis of the LIFO/FIFO calculations.

Quantity. Enter the quantity of the purchase. Do not enter commas; dBXL will do that for you.

Unit cost. If you enter the unit cost for the purchase, the program will compute the Extended Cost (next field). You also have the option of leaving Unit Cost blank and pressing **<ENTER>** to move on to the Extended Cost field. In that case, the program will calculate the unit cost and insert it into the field.

Extended cost. See Unit Cost field.

Supplier #. Enter a valid supplier's number (one that has been entered into a support file record). If the number is valid, the program will search through the supplier support file and insert the supplier's name in the following field. If the number does not exist in the support file, the program will display the following message:

`SUPPLIER NOT FOUND, PRESS ENTER TO CONTINUE`

At this point, you have two options. Either press **<ENTER>** and re-enter the correct number, or exit the Purchase Input screen and create a support file record for the supplier number you wish to input. To exit the program, overwrite whatever you typed in the Supplier # field by pressing the space bar until the field is blank, and press**.** The Main Menu will be displayed, after which you can create a new support-file record.

Name. The supplier's name will be automatically inserted, as explained above in the Supplier # field.

When you press **<ENTER>** in the (supplier) Name field, the bottom of the screen will display the message:

`PROCESS PURCHASE (Y/N)`

If you press **Y**, the record will be appended to the database. (Do not press **<ENTER>** if your system appears to be idle; this process may take a few moments or more to update all indexes, depending on your computer.) Once the record is processed, the cursor will return to the Stock # field. You can enter another purchase transaction, or exit to the Main Menu by leaving the field blank and pressing **<ENTER>.** If you press **N**, the program will return directly to the Main Menu, and your entries will not be added to the database.

Entering Sales Transactions

To enter a customer sales transaction, select Option #2 from the Main Menu. The program will then display the Sales Input screen. The Sales Input screen is divided into two sections.

Inventory Status. Displays the quantity of parts available in inventory.

Customer Order. Contains information about the sale (customer, quantity, price, date).

INVENTORY STATUS SECTION

This section contains the following fields:

Part #. Enter the number of the item that the customer is purchasing. The number must be in the part-number support file. If the number is valid, the description of the part will appear in the next field, Description, and the number in inventory will be displayed in the Avail. Quantity field.

If the number is invalid, the program will indicate that the part number was not found. Either re-enter the correct number or exit the Sales Input screen and create a support file record for the part number you wish to input. (The exit is the same as that used in the Purchase Input screen, above. Erase the field with the Backspace key and enter a blank. You will then return to the Main Menu.)

Description. Filled in by the system (see Part # field, above).

Avail. quantity. Filled in by the system (see Part # field, above).

CUSTOMER ORDER SECTION

Customer #. Enter a customer that has already been input in a support file record. If the number is valid, the program will display the appropriate customer name. If the program can't find the customer, an error message will appear on the lower part of the screen. Either correct the number or exit (same routine as above) and create the necessary support file. Then re-enter the record by selecting Option #2 again from the Main Menu.

Name. Filled in by the system (see Customer #, above).

Sale quantity. Enter the customer's order quantity for the part described above. If the quantity displayed is larger than the on-hand inventory balance, the program will display the following message at the bottom of the screen:

```
INSUFFICIENT QUANTITY ON HAND, PRESS ANY KEY TO CONTINUE
```

The program will then display a new Sales Input screen. You will then have to reinput your previous inventory and customer data.

Unit Price. When you enter the unit price (no commas or dollar signs), the program will automatically compute the extended price (next field). Alternately, you can leave the unit price blank and enter the extended price in the next field. The program will compute the unit price and fill in the amount in the Unit Price field.

Extended price. See Unit Price field, above.

Sale date. Enter the date of the customer's order.

When you press **<ENTER>** after entering the date of the sale, the program will ask if you wish to process the sale. If you respond **Y**, the system will create a sale number in the right portion of the Sales Input screen. Be patient; processing may require a few moments to update all indexes, depending on your computer. Do not press **<ENTER>** to speed things up. If you press N, the program will return to the Main Menu, and the data you entered in the Sales Input screen will be lost.

Editing/Viewing/Deleting Purchase Records, Sales Records, and Support files

The Scan Function

To recall a previously created purchase records, sales record, or support file record, select Option #A, Edit/Delete Records, from the Main Menu. This action will display the Scan Selection Menu.

Scanning is used to search for a record or group of records, and then to display them on the screen. It is useful for two purposes. First, it will enable you to pinpoint a specific record for viewing, editing, or deleting, as explained below. Second, you can locate a group of records and display them one-by-one for editing or deletion.

One way to think of the second scan function is to imagine the records on a track. When you scan for, say all purchase records with Part # A-1000, the program will find the first record that has A-1000 in Part # field. It will then display that record in the scanning format. You can view the rest of the records one after another, forward and backward (by pressing **F** and **B**; see editing options, below). The records will appear alphabetically or numerically in the order determined by the criteria you selected. If you enter a blank scan criteria and press **<ENTER>** or **ESC**, the program will display the first record in the database, according to the criteria you selected.

Scanning Purchase Records

1. Select Option #1 from the Scan Selection Menu. The Purchase Scanning Menu will then be displayed, offering you four criteria for organizing records for viewing or editing (stock #, part #, location, or supplier number).

2. When you select any of the options from the Purchase Scanning Menu, the program will display an input screen, in which you can enter a specific request.. For example, when you select Option #2, Scan Purchases by part #, an input screen appears. If you enter 1023, the program will locate all purchase records in which 1023 appears in the part # field. The records will be organized numerically by part number, and displayed in Scanning Screen format. The same procedure is used for the other scan criteria options available from the Purchase Scanning Menu. Once the records are located, you can view, modify, or delete them using the options described in the Editing Options section, below.

Scanning Sales Record

1. If you select Option #2 from the Scan Selection Menu, the Sales Scanning Menu will be displayed. Choose a scanning criteria (Sale #, Customer #, or Part #).

2. Once you've selected your criteria, an input screen will be displayed. Enter the appropriate data, and press **<ENTER>**. Records matching those criteria will be grouped together for your viewing or editing, in Scanning Screen format.

Scanning Support Files

The scan function can also be used to locate a specific record in your support files. The procedure is:

1. When the Scan Selection Menu is displayed, you will have two options for locating records in the support file. Option #3 allows you to scan a support file by name (e.g., supplier name, customer name, part name), while option #4 is used to scan by number (supplier number, customer number, part number).

2. When you select either option, the program displays the Support File Scanning Menu. Select the desired scan criteria, and an input screen will be displayed. Enter your scan criteria. Once you have found the record you are seeking, use the editing options described below.

If no purchase records, sales records, or support file records match your criteria entered in the input screens, the program will display the following message:

```
No records meet your criteria
Press any key to continue
```

Scanning Options

Whenever records are located through the scan function, they appear in Scanning Screen format. Notice that the bottom of the screen displays a number of options for viewing, editing, or deleting records. These are:

F= Forward, B=Backward. Each time your press **F**, you will browse forward from one record to another. Press **B** to move backward through the file. The program will move backward one record each time the B key is pressed. If you try to scan past the end of the file (the record most recently input), or the beginning of the file (the first record entered), the program will beep and remain on the last record.

E=Edit. Once you have located a record that you would like to alter, select **E** and the program will switch to full screen edit mode. Each field will be highlighted on the screen, just as it was during initial data entry. You can move from highlighted field to highlighted field by using the cursor or pressing **<ENTER>**. Each time you press **<ENTER>**, the cursor will advance one field. Make your changes in a field using the Backspace, Insert, and Delete keys. The editing process is ended by pressing **CTRL-END** in any field, or by pressing **<ENTER>** in the last field. Either action will save the information to disk. You can exit without saving the changes to disk by pressing the **ESC** key.

D=Delete. Deletion with the Inventory Management Program is a two-step process. First, press **D** to mark the record for deletion. MARKED FOR DELETION will then appear above the menu options. Although a record is marked for deletion, it is not actually removed from the database until you use the Pack function, which is accessed from the Utilities Menu (see below). Records may remain in the marked state indefinitely. Even when you exit the program and return at a later date, records slated for deletion will still be marked.

U=Undelete. If you decide that you do not want to delete a marked record and you haven't used the Pack function yet, you can unmark the record by selecting the U option. The MARKED FOR DELETION message will then be removed from the record.

0 =Exit. When you select the **0** option, the program will return to the Main Menu.

Generating Reports

The Inventory Management Program allows you to output your purchase and sales records in summary and detail format. In addition, you can print listings of the contents of your support files. All of the reports will line up properly on 8.5 x 11-inch paper using condensed (15 characters per inch) type.

To begin the report-generation process, select Option #5 from the Main Menu. The Print Menu will then be displayed, offering you the following choices:

1. Print purchases.

2. Print sales.

3. Print support files.

The steps for outputting the two types of reports follow.

Print Purchases

Determine a sort order. After choosing option #1 from the Print Menu, the Sort Order Selection Menu will be displayed. This menu allows you to choose the order in which records will be printed on the reports (stock #, part #, supplier #, or location). For example, if you choose Stock #, the records will be printed in numerical sequence by the stock numbers you assigned during data input.

Indicate the date and status criteria. After you choose a sort order, the program will display the Purchase Report Criteria screen.

1. Enter the starting and ending dates for the purchase records you would like to print.

2. Indicate whether you would like a report of current stock only. If you select Y, the report will exclude any stock purchase that has a remaining balance of zero.

3. If desired, enter a minimum amount below which records will not appear in the report.

4. When you press **<ENTER>** after inputting the minimum amount, the program will search for records that match your criteria. If you wish to terminate the process, press **ESC**. If no records match the search criteria the following message will be displayed:

```
No records meet your criteria
Press any key to continue
```

5. If any records do match your criteria, the program will display a Criteria Search Results screen, which indicates the number of records that met the criteria. Press P to display the Report Selection Menu, or **ESC** to terminate the process and return to the Main Menu.

Choose a report. The Report Selection Menu offers you two different types of purchase reports:

1. Detailed report. Includes all data from the Purchase Input screen.

2. Summary report. Depending on what order you chose from the Sort Order Selection Menu, the summary report will break out items by location, part number, stock number, or supplier number.

Once you have selected the type of report you want to print, a message will prompt you to:

```
Align printer and press return to continue.
```

Make sure your printer is on-line before pressing **<ENTER>**. Otherwise you will get an error message. Retry with your printer on-line.

Print Sales

Determine a sort order. As in the case of printing purchase records, when you choose Print Sales from the Print Menu (Option #2) you will have to determine a sort order for the report. The Sort Order Selection Menu for sales reports offers three options: sale number, part number, and customer number.

Indicate the date and values criteria. After you choose a sort order, the program will display the Sales Report Criteria screen.

1. Enter the starting and ending dates for the sales records you would like to print.

2. If desired, enter a minimum amount below which records will not appear in the report.

3. When you press **<ENTER>** after inputting the minimum amount, the program will search for records that match your criteria.

4. If any records match your criteria, the program will display a Criteria Search Results screen, which indicates the number of records that met the criteria. Press P to display the Report Selection Menu, or **ESC** to terminate the process and return to the Main Menu.

5. The following message will be displayed if no records match the search criteria:

```
No records meet your criteria
Press any key to continue
```

Choose a report. The Report Selection Menu offers two types of sales reports:

1. Detailed report. Includes all data from the Sales Input screen.

2. Summary report. Depending on what order you chose from the Sort Order Selection screen, the summary report will break out items by sale #, customer #, or part #.

Once you have selected the type of report you want to print, a Message screen will prompt you to align the printer. See above for recourse if printing is initiated while printer is off-line.

Print Support File Reports

Choose the report type. When you select Option #3 from the Print Menu, the program will display a Sort Order Selection Menu which offers you two types of support file reports.

1. Support files by name. Outputs all data on each support record, organized by the supplier, customer, or part name that was input on each record.

2. Support files by number. Same as above, but organizes reports by the supplier, customer, or part number input on each record.

Select the support file you wish to print. Once you select a report type, the program will display the Support File Report Selection Menu. The menu offers you options for printing all three types of support files (customer, part, supplier).

Using Utilities

The Inventory Management Program includes three housekeeping functions for maintaining the database. These are accessed from the Utilities Menu, which you used earlier to set up the program. The Utilities Menu is accessed by selecting Option #6 from the Main Menu. The utility options are described below.

Reindex. Occasionally, you may find that the search routines are not operating correctly. The most probable cause for this is a damaged index. This usually results from illegally exiting the program (see the discussion on exiting, below, for the proper exit routine). If this should occur, you must reindex the files by selecting Option #1 from the Utilities Menu. The reindexing option will take a variable period of time, depending on the number of records in the file and the type of computer you are using.

Pack. Packing is the final stage used to delete marked records (see Editing Records). Unlike marking a record, though, packing is an irreversible action; once a record is packed, it no longer exists. After selecting the pack option, the program will display how many records will be packed, and you will be asked to confirm your choice with a **Y** plus **<ENTER>**. The packing process can take several minutes or longer since it must update all indexes.

System setup. The Inventory Program uses all dBXL To Go basic setup options. These are described in chapter 1.

Accounting (L) IFO/(F) IFO. LIFO stands for Last in, first out, while FIFO means First in, first out. Let's say you have purchased more than one lot of a given part on different dates. Under LIFO, when a sale is made the program will draw from inventory the most recently purchased lots. Under the FIFO setup option, inventory would be drawn from the oldest lots. The choice has accounting ramifications, and should be made on the basis of your company's current accounting practices.

Note: If you want to delete all records and start with a clean database, you can either recopy the .dbf files from your distribution diskette or use the dBXL Zap command to erase all records. Zap simultaneously deletes and packs all records in your database. To use Zap, make current the directory in which you keep your Inventory Program files. Start dBXL, and then at the prompt type:

```
use warebuy
```

Next, type:

```
zap
```

dBXL will ask you to confirm the action with **Y** or **N**. When you select **Y**, all records will be erased and deleted from your database. Repeat this procedure for the remaining database programs: wareclnt, warepart, waresale, and waresupl. After zapping the databases, you must reindex to ensure that your indexes correspond to the program.

> **CAUTION**: Zap is an irrevocable command; there is no way to recover a zapped file. Therefore, back up your data before zapping it!

Exiting

It is vitally important that you properly exit from the Inventory Program. Failure to do so may cause file or index damage. While it is often possible to remedy the situation by reindexing, the damage may be permanent, in which case you must start over again by copying the files from your working diskette and re-entering your data, or restoring your database from your most recent backup copy. Given the needless waste of time and the aggravation in reconstructing a database, always exit by pressing **0** in the menu you are working with until you reach the Main Menu. Pressing **0** at the Main Menu will close all database files and return to a Sign-off screen that asks you if you wish to leave the program. Entering **Y** returns you to DOS. Entering **N** returns you to the Main Menu. Note: If you are running an uncompiled program, pressing **X** will return you to the dBXL prompt.

5 Manual For Note Card Program

Features

- Menu driven.
- Password protection.
- Enables user to create electronic index cards for business, academic, or personal note keeping.
- Allows for user-defined codes that can be used to organize and retrieve selected cards.
- Sorts note cards by codes, topics, subjects, and key words.
- Generates reports of complete or selected note cards in order of selected criteria.
- Permits notes of unlimited length without the inefficiencies of a flat-file storage system.

Contents

Introduction

This program enables you to develop and maintain a comprehensive note card file. Each note card can include a topic, subject, two selection codes, key words, description, comments, and a memo. Additionally, each card may be numbered and ordered in any sequence you choose. The note card system has numerous applications, ranging from cataloging marketing and sales data to creating project memos and recipes. The uses are only limited by your imagination.

The Note Card Program is extremely flexible, and allows you to create a relational structure that suits your specific needs. An open-ended memo field is available for each note card, and offers features such as automatic word wrap, full-screen edit, and format control. Any notecards you create may be sorted by criteria you specify. You can also generate six types of reports, including:

1. Summary report. Prints compact version of all note cards.

2. Detailed report. Prints out all information (except the text) as it was entered into the database.

3. Memo report. Prints all note card text.

4. Topic report. Organizes the note cards by subject within topic headings.

5. Subject report. Organizes the note cards by subject.

6. Subject within topic report. Outputs note cards by topic headings, then by subject headings.

All functions of the program are accessed by menus that include instructions on the bottom of the screen. These menus allow you to: customize the note card report header and printer specifications, establish passwords, scan records, print reports, and update the note card file using various utilities and edit functions.

Before using the program, read through this manual and familiarize yourself with all the input, report, and utility functions. You may want to set up a practice note card system, using two or three note cards to review the functions of the program. Also, create a backup disk for your database and memo files (note.dbf and note.dbt). There's no need to back up your program (.prg), format (.fmt), or report (.frm) files. You can always recopy them from your working diskette. You don't have to back up your index files either, since your program creates them if they aren't found in the directory.

At a minimum, back up your .dbf and .dbt files each time you add or edit records; the few minutes that the procedure requires will more than offset the time you would need to spend if the entire database had to be recreated. Remember, no hardware system is infallible, and it's better to be safe than sorry!

Finally, if you are an experienced dBXL user and wish to modify the program, refer to the Technical Appendix charts and tables. You will find a program tree that lists the calling program hierarchy, a table that describes each index file, and a list of files required to run the program.

Data Entry Keys

After you have input data, you may use the Backspace key to erase the characters, if you want to edit your entry (provided that you haven't pressed **<ENTER>**). Alternately, you can use the cursor and Delete/Insert keys to modify your entry. When you do press **<ENTER>**, the cursor will move to the next data input field. If you need to return to a previous entry, use the up cursor key to move the cursor to the field. Enter your changes and press **<ENTER>** to move on through the input screen. Note that any errors made during data entry can also be corrected later by means of the Edit option (see below).

Installing and Setting up the Program

Before you begin using the Note Card Program, you will have to install and set it up. General instructions for installation and setup are contained in Chapter 1.

Starting the Program

The easiest way to start the Note Card Program is to create a batch file. You can also start the program manually by typing

```
do note
```

after starting dBXL (see Chapter 1, for specifics of both startup techniques).

Regardless of how you begin the Note Card Program, you will first see the dBXL copyright and license notice. The screen will display the message "Creating indexes, please wait." This process may require a few seconds, but only occurs the first time you run the program after installation. The Note Card Program Main Menu will then appear.

Creating Note Cards

All data is entered through the Note Card Input screen, which is called up by selecting Option #1, Add Records, from the Main Menu. The screen consists of two sections.

Topic/Identification section. Provides fields for topic and subject, as well as user-defined codes and a user-defined sequence for ordering records. Also provides entry point for Text (memo) field.

Description section. Source information and user comment, as well as entry point for text.

Topic/Indentification Section

When you select Add Records from the Main Menu, the cursor will move through the following sequence of fields each time you press <ENTER>.

Text (memo). On the Note Card Input screen you will notice that the Text (memo) field appears in two places: in the top left and the bottom left corners of your screen. This enables you to input a memo for a note card either before or after you input the rest of the information.

To enter a memo, press **CTRL-PgDn** when the cursor is in the highlighted field occupied by the word *memo*. The dBXL Text Editor Help Screen will replace the input screen, and the cursor will be under the left corner of the Help Screen border. You can type as much text as you wish. The text editing functions are listed in the Help Screen. (Note: If you are a WordStar user, you will be right at home with the dBXL text editing commands). Consult your dBXL manual for additional details on the use of the text editor.

When you have finished entering the text, press **CTRL-END** or **CTRL-W**. This will add the memo into the database and return the cursor back to the Note Card Input screen. If you wish to exit the memo without saving it, press **ESC**. dBXL will then prompt you as to whether you wish to abort editing. Respond by typing **Y**.

Topic. Enter the broadest general category that covers the topic you are investigating. Let's say you're doing market research on gourmet frozen dinners. You might list the topic as **GOURMET TV DINNERS**. Be as consistent as possible each time you input the topic, so that all like topics will be grouped together on reports.

Subject. Enter the specific subject you are researching or tracking. If the topic is Gourmet TV Dinners, the subject might be Consumer Demographics. The consistency rules for the Topic field apply to this field as well.

Key words. You may enter up to four key words that identify the content of the note card. Separate each key word with a space. You can later use the report generator to select those note cards that have one or more of the words input in the Key Word field. For the subject Consumer Demographics, you might find a source that lists Baby Boomers. You might enter Boomer as a keyword. Likewise you might enter the key word Yuppy. Later you can pull together all records that mention Boomer and Yuppy. Once again, consistency is important; if you do not enter exact spelling and abbreviations, you will either fail to group together all like records on reports, or you'll wind up with reports that contain unrelated records.

Code 1/Code 2. These two fields are user-defined, and give you a powerful and flexible system for tagging and retrieving records. It is well worth your time to plan how you will use the codes, because a well thought-out code system will enable you to accomplish a wide variety of information management tasks.

Let's say you're conducting a market research survey on gourmet frozen foods. Your information sources include magazine articles, advertisements, and interviews. You might use Code 1 to indicate the source type. For example, the code P could refer to a periodical article, I might indicate that the information came from an interview with an industry expert, and A might indicate that an advertisement was the source.

Code 2 might be used to describe the nature of the note card: S might be statistical information, B might be brand-specific information, P might be sales projections, and O might be overview. Conceivably, a Code 2 entry might include more than one description; PO could be used to indicate a note card that not only has overview information, but has market projections. Similarly, PB could indicate a card with sales or market share projections for a particular brand.

In general, the simpler the coding system, the less chance there is of consistency errors. If you choose Stat instead of S for statistics, someone may accidentally input Stats (plural). As far as dBXL is concerned, Stat and Stats are completely different entities that will be grouped separately in reports. Hint: Keep a list of codes and abbreviations by your computer. This will minimize the chances of entering wrong or inconsistent coding information.

Order. The Order field allows you to specify a unique order in which the note cards will appear in reports. For example, even though you might be randomly entering your research findings into individual notes, you might want to output them in a specific sequence later. To do so, create a numbering system with the Order field. It is best to start with multiples of 10. This will allow you to insert records between adjacent notes. You can also use the decimal place to insert more notes (10.1, 10.2, 10.3, etc.). When you select order as a means for organizing reports (see Generating Reports, below), the notes will be printed out according to your scheme.

Description Section

Source. This field can be used to briefly describe the information source, such as a magazine article, a newspaper clipping, or a telephone interview. For example, if you interviewed an industry expert, you might list his or her name and phone number. You can skip this field if it is not relevant, or alter its meaning to suit your needs.

Comment. The Comment field can contain an all-purpose statement about the content of the card or the source. For example, if you cited, *Business Monthly,* Feb 87, as the source for a card, you might enter comments such as "Good source of numbers," or "Supports Bill Hopewell's theory." Note that the cursor will not wrap like a word processor. That means you must press **<ENTER>** to move the cursor to the next line. If you begin typing a word and find that it breaks in an incorrect place for a hyphen, use the Backspace or cursor and Delete keys to modify your entry. The comment field is not used for searches or sorts.

Text (memo). This field is identical to the Text (memo) field described above. Press **CTRL-PgDn** to create a text memo, **CTRL-END** or **CTRL-W** to save the text, or **ESC** to abandon the text without saving it. The reason Text (memo) appears twice on the screen, as the first and last fields, is that logically you might want to enter a memo after you have input the identification and description information. When you later edit or view a record on screen, however, you do not want to have to press **<ENTER>** nine times before you can press **CTRL-PgDn** and display the memo. Hence the dual position of the field.

Adding Another Note Card

When you press **<ENTER>** while the cursor is in the second Text (memo) field, or press **CTRL-END** elsewhere during data input, the record will be included in the database. A prompt at the bottom of the screen will then ask if you want to add another record. To accept the default Y and continue adding records, press **<ENTER>**. If you enter N, the program will return to the Main Menu.

Editing/Viewing/Deleting Note Cards

The Scan Function

To recall a previously created note card, select the Edit/Delete Records option from the Main Menu (Option #2), then choose from the Edit/Delete Menu a criteria by which you will scan for records in the database.

Scanning is used to search for a record or group of records, and then to display them on the screen. It is useful for two purposes. First, it enables you to pinpoint a specific record for viewing, editing, or deleting, as explained below. Second, you can locate a group of records, and display them one by one for editing or deletion.

One way to think of the second scan function is to imagine the records on a track. When you scan for all articles with Consumer Demographics as a subject, the program will find the first record that has those words in the Subject field. It will then display that record in the scanning format (see below). You can view the rest of the records one after another, forward and backward (by pressing **F** and **B**; see editing options, below). The records will appear in an order determined by the criteria you selected; alphabetical order for alphabetic fields, such as Topic, Subject, and Numeric for the Order field.

Scanning Procedures

The following process is identical for each scan option:

1. Select the criteria field on which you want to scan for records. The Scanning Criteria Input screen will then be displayed. Enter the appropriate information. You can use contractions of the name you are seeking and the program will find the first record matching the contraction. For example, if you only enter C for a scan by name, the program will display the first record starting with the letter.

2. If any note cards match the word(s) or contraction(s) you entered, the record you are seeking will be displayed in a special Scanning Screen format. Once the record is in Scanning Screen format, you can use any of the editing, viewing, or deletion options described

below. If there is more than one record for the name or word you input, the program will display the first one entered. If you entered an abbreviation or contraction of a name or word, the program will display records in the order determined by the entire field. For example, if you scan on Tel in the subject field, records with Telephone and Television will be found. Telephone will appear first, though, because it alphabetically precedes Television.

3. If no records in the database match the name or word entered in the Scanning Criteria Input screen, the program will display the following message:

    ```
    No records meet your criteria.
    Press any key to continue
    ```

4. If you enter a blank and press <ENTER> in the Scanning Criteria Input screen, the first record in the database will be displayed. You can then page through the database using the Forward option described below. Note: You can also move to the first record in the database by leaving the input screen blank and pressing **ESC.**

Scanning Options

Once you have located the desired record(s), you can use any of the functions listed at the bottom of the Scanning Screen.

T =Text. If you select **T**, the program will redisplay the Scanning screen, this time with a highlighted memo field. You can edit or view the memo by pressing **CTRL-PGDN**. When you have made the necessary changes, press **CTRL-END** or **CTRL-W**. If you have only viewed the memo, or decided that you don't want to save the changes, press **ESC** and the record will reappear in full screen text edit mode. Press **ESC** again to return to the generic Scanning Screen format. Press **ESC** once more to return to the Main Menu.

F = Forward, B = Backward. Each time your press **F**, the program will browse forward from one record to another. To move backward through the file, press B. The program will move backward one record each time the B key is pressed. If you try to scan past the end of the file (the record most recently input) or the beginning of the file (the first record entered), the program will beep and remain on the last (or first) record.

E = Edit. Once you have located a record for editing through the Scan option, select item **E**. The program will then enter full screen edit mode, in which each field will be highlighted on the screen as it was during initial data entry. You can move from highlighted field to highlighted field by using the cursor or pressing <ENTER>. Each time you press return, the cursor will advance one field. Make your changes in a field using the Backspace, Insert, and Delete keys. The editing process is ended by pressing **CTRL-END** in any field, or by pressing <ENTER> in the last field, Text (memo). Either action will save the information to disk. To edit the text field, place the cursor on the Memo field and press **CTRL-PgDn**. You can exit without saving the changes to disk by pressing the **ESC** key.

D = Delete. Deletion with the Note Card Program is a two-step process. First, press **D** to mark the record for deletion. MARKED FOR DELETION will appear near the bottom of the screen. Although a record is marked for deletion, it is not actually erased until you use the Pack function, which is accessed from the Utilities Menu (see below). Records may remain in the marked state indefinitely. Even when you exit the program and return at a later date, records slated for deletion will still be marked.

U=Undelete. If you decide that you don't want to delete a record and you haven't used the Pack function yet, you can unmark the record for deletion by selecting the **U** option. The MARKED FOR DELETION message will then be removed from your screen.

0=Exit. When you select the **0** option, the program will return to the Main Menu.

Generating Reports

The Note Card Program uses a number of formats and organizing schemes to print your records. All of the reports will line up properly on 8.5 x 11 inch paper using condensed (15 characters per inch) type. To create any of the reports, select the Generate Reports option (#3) from the Main Menu. The Print Menu will then be displayed offering you two options:

1. Print entire database.

2. Print selected records.

Print Entire Database

1. If you choose Print Entire Database, a Sort Order Selection Menu will be displayed. Choose the option by which you want the report sorted. Once the sort order is selected, the Report Selection Menu will be displayed (see below for a description of report options). Be sure to select a sort option that is logical for the report you wish to generate. For example, you should probably select the Topic sort order for the Topic Report, and the Subject sort for the Subject Report; otherwise, you may generate confusing reports. In some cases, however, crossing reports with various sort orders can produce valuable special reports. Experiment and determine which combinations provide the most useful information for you.

2. Select the kind of report you want from the Report Selection Menu, which offers the following options:

    Summary Report. Contains the topic, subject, codes, order, and key words, source, and comments. Memo text is printed in a separate report (see below). The Summary Report prints eight note cards per page. (Suggested sort order: any.)

    Detailed report. Presents the same information as the Summary Report, but it is displayed exactly as it appears on the screen, two per page. Use this report when you need space between entries to annotate or edit your entries. (Suggested sort order: any.)

Memo report. Prints the full memo text for each record. The left side of the report shows the topic and subject, while the memo is printed on the right side. (Suggested sort order: any.)

Topic report. Organizes your note cards by topic. For example, all records that have the topic Gourmet TV Dinners would be printed under that topic heading. Within each topic, note cards are organized alphabetically by subject. (Suggested sort order: Topic.)

Subject report. Prints out note cards by subject headings. All cards with the same headings will be grouped together and listed alphabetically, provided they have been input consistently. (Suggested sort order: Subject.).

Subject within topic report. Groups together all note cards with the same topic, provided they have been input consistently. Within each topic, similar subjects are subgrouped together and listed alphabetically. Each topic starts at the top of a new page. If you would rather have a continuous printout, select Topic Report, described above. (Suggested sort order: Topic.)

3. Once you have selected the type of report you want to print, a message screen will prompt you to:

```
Align printer and press return to continue.
```

Make sure your printer is on-line before pressing **<ENTER>**. Otherwise you will get an error message. Retry with your printer on-line.

Print Selected Records

This option from the Print Menu allows you to select specific kinds of records to be printed. Take the following steps:

1. When you press 2, the Report Criteria Input screen will be displayed. Notice that the Report Criteria Input screen is identical to the input screens you used to input and edit records, with the exception that only certain fields are highlighted. You can select the records you want to filter from the database by indicating your criteria in the highlighted fields. For example, entering B in the Type field will print all records with B in that field. If you wanted to further refine the list you might specify BOOMER and YUPP in the Key Word fields. This will only print out note cards that refer to Baby Boomers and Yuppies. (Since the program seeks matches only for the letters entered, YUPP will find Yuppy as well as Yuppies.) Note that any field left blank will *not* be included in the filter.

One caveat: A record must meet *all* your search criteria to pass through the filter. So if you make the selection filter too fine by adding too many criteria, you will probably not print any records at all. Unfortunately, there is no absolute number of criteria above which the filter function defeats itself; each database has its own limits. With a little experimenting, however, you will quickly determine the maximum productive levels of criteria that can be used for your data.

Note that the Key Words field is split into four separate fields on the Criteria screen, but that on the Note Card Input screen you entered the words in one large field. Some of the words you originally entered in the record may be too long to fit into one of the four fields. Don't worry—a match is made on the basis of whatever letters are entered, so you will most likely locate the records you are seeking. If you enter more than one key word in the Report Criteria screen, a record must match *both* words to be included.

Finally, one field deserves special attention: Order. Note that Order is displayed as two fields, separated by a dash. This allows you to print a range of records; for example, records numbered 100 through 120. If you want to capture records with all Order numbers, leave the field blank.

Once you have entered the criteria by which you wish to filter the database, press **CTRL-END**, or press **<ENTER>** in the last highlighted field. The Sort Order Selection Menu described above will be displayed. Choose the order by which you want records to be located and printed. The program will then look for records that match the criteria you input, and create a report from them.

2. If any records match your criteria, the program will display the Criteria Search Results screen, which indicates how many records meet your criteria. The Criteria Search Results Screen gives you the following options:

    ***Press* P *to print*.** Use this option if you wish to print out the selected records. You will be presented with the Report Selection Menu described above. The menu will indicate how many records are to be printed, along with criteria you used to select them. The report formats are the same as those used to print the entire database (see below). Note that when reports are printed out after a criteria search, the criteria used will be indicated at the top of the page.

    ***Press* S *to display on screen*.** Before you print a report, you may want to view the note cards first to make sure you have retrieved the correct one(s). Or, you may just wish to review the selected records on the screen. This option allows you to do either. When you press **S**, the screen will display the first note card that met your search criteria in Scanning Screen format. If more than one record was found, you can page forward and backward through the selected records by using the **F** (forward) and **B** (backward). The principle is the same as that used in the editing process described above.

    To view a memo, press **T** (text). The screen will then be redisplayed, with the word *memo* highlighted in the Memo field. Press **CTRL-PgDn** and the memo will be displayed. When you are done viewing the memo, press **ESC** or **CTRL-END**.

After you are finished examining the selected records, press 0 to return to the Report Selection Menu. You can then print the selected records, or return to the Main Menu by pressing 0.

3. If no records are located, the program displays the message:

```
No records meet your criteria
Press any key to continue
```

The program will then return to the Main Menu.

Using Utilities

The Note Card Program includes four housekeeping functions. These are accessed from the Utilities Menu, which you used earlier to set up the program. The Utilities Menu is accessed by selecting Option #4 from the Main Menu. The housekeeping options are described below.

Reindex. Occasionally, you may find that the search routines are not operating correctly. The most probable cause for this is a damaged index. This usually results from illegally exiting the program (see below for the proper exit routine). If this should occur, you must reindex the files by selecting Option #1 from the Utilities Menu. The reindexing option will take a variable period of time, depending on the number of records in the file and the type of computer you are using.

Pack. Packing is the final stage used to delete marked records (see Editing/Viewing/Deleting Note Cards, above). Unlike marking a record, though, packing is an irreversible action; once a note card is packed, it no longer exists. After selecting the pack option, the program will display how many records will be packed, and you will be prompted to confirm your choice with a Y plus a <**ENTER**>. The packing process can take several minutes or longer, since it must update all indexes.

System setup. The Note Card Program uses the dBXL To Go basic setup options. These are described in Chapter 1.

Note: If you want to delete all records and start with a clean database, you can either recopy the .dbf files from your distribution diskette or use the dBXL **Zap** command to erase all records. **Zap** simultaneously deletes and packs all records in your database. To use **Zap**, make current the directory in which you keep your Note Card Program files. Start dBXL, and then at the prompt type:

```
use note
```

Next, type:

```
zap
```

dBXL will ask you to confirm the action with a **Y** or **N**. When you select **Y**, all records will be erased and deleted from your database. After zapping, you must reindex to ensure that your indexes correspond to the program.

> **CAUTION: Zap** is an irrevocable command, and there is no way to recover a zapped file. Therefore, back up your data before zapping it!

Exiting

It is vitally important that you properly exit from the Note Card Program. Failure to do so may cause file or index damage. While it is often possible to remedy the situation by reindexing, the damage may be permanent, in which case you must start over again by copying the files from your working diskette and re-entering your data, or restoring your database from your most recent backup copy. Given the needless waste of time and the aggravation in reconstructing a database, *always exit by pressing 0 in the menu you are working with until you reach the Main Menu.* Pressing **0** at the Main Menu will close all database files and return you to a Sign-Off screen that asks you if you wish to leave the program. Entering **Y** returns you to DOS. Entering **N** returns you to the Main Menu. Note: If you are running an uncompiled program, pressing **X** will return you to the dBXL prompt.

6 Mailing List Management Program

Features

- Menu driven.
- Password protection.
- Complete system for creating, maintaining, and outputting mailing lists.
- Auto-entry features assist in entering repetitive information.
- Program automatically indicates previous five times a mailing record has been used.
- User-selectable titles and codes for mailing labels.
- Sorts and outputs labels by name, company, zip, or state.
- Supports most common pressure-sensitive and cheshire label configurations.

Contents

Introduction

The Mailing List Management Program is a complete system for building and maintaining mailing lists. It is ideal for small businesses that market through direct mail and compile lists through customer response cards (warranty information, surveys, etc.) or through research into public domain sources. Nonprofit organizations will also find it helpful for creating fund raiser mailing lists. Finally, while the program is not intended to be used in lieu of a stand-alone membership or subscription maintenance system, the code field can be used to indicate whether an individual is active or inactive, or falls into some other relevant status.

The Mailing List Management Program makes it easy to quickly enter large batches of mailing list records, and can automatically insert repetitive information in user-selected fields. Once mailing list records have been entered into the system, you can output them in a variety of label formats, including:

1. One up, pressure-sensitive (3 $^1/_2$" x $^{15}/_{16}$" and 4 $^1/_5$" x 1 $^7/_{16}$")

2. Three up, pressure-sensitive

3. Four up cheshire

Each time you output a list, you can assign a list code or add a title of your choice (Owner, President, etc.). You can also create a hardcopy of your mailing list through the summary report.

A unique feature of this program is that it allows you to assign attribute codes to a record, rather than merely assigning a name to a list. Later, you can temporarily assign the name to a list based on the attributes (e.g., people who purchased a specific item, people who fall within a certain demographic group, etc.). When you wish to output a mailing list, you can then group together all records that have the desired attributes, and create a unique list. The system thus creates "virtual mailing lists" that are subsets of the total database and exist only for output sake.

The advantage is that you can use the records in as many different lists as you like. You can also instruct the program to include certain names that were used in previous mailings, thus drawing on historical knowledge of mailing performance. The usage monitor field in each record indicates the previous five times that a particular record was included in a list. With this mechanism, you can precisely track the contexts in which a particular name has been used. Conversely, the program's selection criteria feature can be used to exclude records from the current list based either on its attributes or prior usage.

Before using the program, read through this manual and familiarize yourself with all the input, report, and utility functions. You may want to set up a practice mailing list system using a dozen or so mailing list records to review the functions of the program. Also, create a backup disk for your database file (Mail.dbf). there's no need to back up your program (.prg), format (.fmt), or report (.frm) files. You can always recopy them from your working diskette.

You don't have to back up your index files either, since your program creates them if they aren't found in the directory

At a minimum, back up your .dbf files each time you add or edit records; the few minutes that the procedure requires will more than offset the time you would need to spend if the entire database had to be recreated. Remember, no hardware system is infallible, and it's better to be safe than sorry!

Finally, if you are an experienced dBXL user and wish to modify the program, refer to the Technical Appendix charts and tables. You will find a program tree that lists the calling program hierarchy, a table that describes each index file, and a list of files required to run the program.

Data Entry Keys

After you have input data, you may use the Backspace key to erase your entry (provided that you haven't pressed **<ENTER>**). Alternately, you can use the cursor and Delete/Insert keys to modify your entry. When you do press **<ENTER>**, the cursor will move to the next data input field. If you need to return to a previous entry, use the up cursor key to move the cursor to the desired field. Enter your changes and press **<ENTER>** to move on through the input screen. Note that any errors made during data entry can also be corrected later by means of the Edit option (see below).

Installing and Setting up the Program

Before you begin using the Mailing List Management Program, you will have to install and set it up. General instructions for installation and setup are in Chapter 1.

Starting the Program

The easiest way to start the Mailing List Management Program is to create a batch file. You can also start the program manually by typing

```
do mail
```

after starting dBXL (see Chapter 1 for specifics of both start-up techniques).

Regardless of how you begin the Mailing List Management Program, you will first see the dBXL copyright and license notice. The screen will display the message "Creating indexes, please wait." This process may require a few seconds, but only occurs the first time you run the program after installation. Mailing List Program Main Menu will then appear.

Adding a Mailing List Record

All data is entered into the database through the Mailing List Input screen, which includes the following fields:

1. Name(s): Three fields are available: Personal Title (Mr., Ms., Mrs., Dr., etc.),First Name Middle Initial, and Last Name

2. Title:

3. Department

4. Company:

5. Address:

6. City

7. State

8. Zip: (up to 10 digits)

9. Country:

10. Telephone:

11. Attributes: Use this field to enter coding descriptions of the addressee. You may enter a maximum of five four-digit codes. For example, 003 might represent IBM AT owners. The code 55K might be people whose annual salary is at least $55,000, while VPM might be used to indicate people at the vice-president level whose area of responsibility is marketing. Let's say all three codes were placed in John Smith's record. Later you could assign Mr. Smith's label to a mailing list targeted to executive computer users, or perhaps to a list of computer users in the marketing field.

    The attribute field could be used just as easily to code records for nonprofit fundraising operations. You could, for example, code income brackets and past philanthropic history, including donation amounts and frequency.

    Associations could assign codes for active members versus inactive members. These codes could then be used to include the lists in appropriate mailings (e.g., membership renewals, special letters to recalcitrant dues payers, etc.).

    Finally, a small publication could devise a coding scheme that indicates a subscriber's status. The expiration month could also be coded, so that once a month a report could be generated, grouping together all subscribers who should receive renewal notices.

    The possibilities are virtually unlimited. Whatever coding scheme you devise, bear two issues in mind. First, take some time to work out the hierarchy and details so that you can assemble lists that truly meet your direct mail needs. If you or the computer operator simply enter codes on the fly, you will have a haphazard system with questionable accuracy and power. This leads to the second issue: consistency. It is vitally important that codes be entered the same way each time. dBXL considers spaces and punctuation marks to be valid characters. Therefore, code 001 is treated very differently from 01 or 0 01.

The best way to ensure consistent usage and entry of codes is a solid game plan for establishing base codes, and a grammar for creating new ones. Keep the coding information near the computer so that all operators know the rules.

12. Usage: Do not enter data in this field; the program does it for you. At the time of list creation, the program inputs the list code in this field (if the record was included in the list being generated).

Accessing the Mailing List Input Screen

To call up the Mailing List Input screen and enter data, select Option #l from the Main Menu. Notice that the first screen you encounter is not called the Mailing List Input screen but the Default Input screen. This screen allows you to fix certain fields for the duration of the data entry session. For example, if everyone's title that you will be entering is Product Manager, or all addresses are in Ohio, you can set the Title and State fields to those designations.

When the Default Input screen appears, enter the desired words or numbers in any of the fields that you would like to remain stationary. When you press <ENTER> in the last field, the Mailing List Input screen will appear with the fields fixed according to your designation. (A shortcut is to press **CTRL-END** at any point in the data input process; this will immediately call up the Mailing List Input screen.)

If you do not want to temporarily fix any fields, simply press **CTRL-END** or **ESC** when the Default Input screen first appears. The Mailing List Input screen will then be displayed without any defaults.

Adding Another Mailing List Record

You can enter data into the Mailing List Input screen in the same fashion as the Default Input screen. If you press <ENTER> when the cursor is in the Attributes field or press **CTRL-END** elsewhere during data input, the record will be included in the database. Each record must have at least a last name or company name to be considered valid and to be added to the database. If you designated one or more fields in the Default Value screen, each new input screen will contain the specified defaults. If you wish to change a specific value for a given record, you can simply overwrite the default value. After each entry, you will be asked if you wish to enter another record. Press <ENTER> to continue or **N** to stop. You will then be asked if you want to change the default values and start data entry again. Press **Y** to change the defaults, or **N** to return to the Main Menu.

Editing/Viewing/Deleting Records

The Scan Function

To recall a previously created mailing list record, select the Edit/Delete Records option from the Main Menu (Option #2), and choose a criterion by which you will scan for records in the database. The scanning criteria for the mailing list program are Name, Company, State, and Zip.

Scanning is used to search for a record or group of records, and then to display them on the screen. It is useful for two purposes. First, it will enable you to pinpoint a specific record for viewing, editing, or deleting, as explained below. Second, you can locate a group of records and display them one-by-one for editing or deletion.

One way to think of the second scan function is to imagine the records on a track. When you scan for all records with the attribute code 001, the program will find the first record that has that designation in the Attribute field. It will then display that record in Scanning Format (see below). You can view them one after another, forward and backward (by pressing **F** and **B**; see editing, below). The records will appear alphabetically in the order determined by the criteria you selected. If you enter a blank scan criteria and press **<ENTER>** or **ESC**, the program will display the first record in the database, according to the criteria you selected.

Scanning Procedures

The following process is identical for each scan option.

1. Select the criteria field on which you want to scan for records. The Scanning Criteria Input screen will then be displayed. Enter the appropriate information. Be as precise as possible, or you may not locate the mailing list records you are seeking. (The consistency issues discussed above apply to locating codes as well as creating codes!) You can use contractions of the name you are seeking and the program will find the first record matching the contractions. For example, if you only enter C for a scan by name, the program will display the first record starting with the letter C.

2. If any mailing list records match the word(s) or contraction(s) you entered, the record you are seeking will be displayed. If there is more than one record for the name or word you entered, the program will display the first one entered. You can then use one of the options described below to edit, view, or delete the information. If you entered an abbreviation or contraction of the actual field, the order will be based on the entire field. For example, if you scan on West in the name field, the program will display records with Westfall and Westlake, as both match the criteria. The one with Westfall will appear first though, because it alphabetically precedes Westlake.

3. If no mailing list records in the database match the name or word entered in the scan input screen, the program will display the following message:

```
No records meet your criteria.
Press any key to continue
```

Scanning Options

Once you have located the desired mailing list record(s), you can use any of the functions listed at the bottom of the Scanning screen.

F = Forward, B = Backward. Each time your press **F**, you will browse forward from one mailing list record to another. To move backward through the file, press **B**. The program will move backward one record each time the B key is pressed. If you try to scan past the end of the file (the record most recently input), or the beginning of the file (the first record entered), the program will beep and remain on the **last** or **first** record.

E=Edit. Once you have located a mailing list record for editing through the Scan option, select item **E**, and the program will enter full screen edit mode. Each field will be highlighted on the screen. You can move from highlighted field to highlighted field by using the cursor or pressing **<ENTER>**. Each time you press **<ENTER>**, the cursor will advance one field. Make your changes in a field using the Backspace, Insert, and Delete keys. The editing process is ended by pressing **CTRL-END** in any field, or by pressing **<ENTER>** in the last field (Attributes). Either action will save the information to disk. You can exit without saving the changes to disk by pressing the **ESC** key.

D=Delete. Deletion with the Mailing List Management Program is a two-step process. First, press **D** to mark the record for deletion. MARKED FOR DELETION will then appear on the lower part of the Scanning Screen. Although a record is marked for deletion, it is not actually deleted until you use the Pack function, which is accessed from the Utilities Menu (see below). Records may remain in the marked state indefinitely. Even when you exit the program and return at a later date, records slated for deletion will still be marked.

U=Undelete. If you decide that you don't want to delete a record and you haven't used the Pack function yet, you can unmark the record for deletion by selecting the U option. The MARKED FOR DELETION message will then be removed from your screen.

0 = Exit. When you select the **0** option, the program will return to the Main Menu.

Generating Reports

The Mailing List Management Program has a number of output formats for mailing labels and reports. All the labels and reports will line up properly using normal or condensed print (10 or 15 characters per inch). Make sure to set the proper condensed print code through the setup option (see Chapter 1). To output labels or create any of the reports, select Option #3, **Generate Reports,** from the Main Menu. The Print Menu will then be displayed, offering you two options:

1. Print entire database.

2. Print selected records.

Print Entire Database

The following steps are taken to print all the records you have entered:

1. When you choose Print Entire Database from the Print Menu, the Sort Order Selection screen will be displayed. Choose the option by which you want the report sorted (Last Name, Company, State, Zip). Once the sort order is selected, the Report Selection Menu will be displayed (see below for options). Be sure to select a sort option that is logical for the report you wish to generate.

2. Select the kind of report you want from the Report Selection Menu, which offers the following options for printing labels and reports:

   LABELS

   A. $3\,{}^{1}/_{2}$" x ${}^{15}/_{16}$"   one across

   B. $3\,{}^{1}/_{2}$" x ${}^{15}/_{16}$"   three across

   C. 4" x $1\,{}^{7}/_{16}$"   one across

   D. $3\,{}^{1}/_{2}$" x ${}^{15}/_{16}$"   cheshire, four across

   REPORTS

   Summary report. Contains a one-line listing of each record, showing the following fields: Name, Company, City, State, Zip, and Attributes. This report is especially useful for checking duplicate entries. (Suggested sort order: any.)

   Detailed report. Prints all data entered on the screen for each record.

   Specification Report. Provides a hard copy record of an assembled list. When you select this report, your printer will generate a hard copy of the screen that you can keep on file as part of the mailing history.

   ASCII. This option outputs one-up labels in ASCII format to a user-named file with a .txt extension. You can then export the file to another program or save it for later printing.

Update records. After you have printed a report or set of labels, you can mark or tag each record used in the list with a four-digit list code (see #3, below).

Each record can keep track of the last five lists it was used on. You can use this usage record to either include or exclude the record from future lists via the Report Criteria Input screen (see Print Selected Records, below).

3. Once you have selected one of the above report options, you will be presented with a List Identification Input screen. This asks you to input a list code (which will be printed on the right side of the label) and a name for the mailing list (for your record keeping purposes). In addition, you will be asked whether you want to suppress the name field, and whether you want to replace the title with one of your own choosing. The latter two options are used when you wish to address a label as President, General Manager, and so on, without a name. Often your source information will only consist of a company name, with no specific name or title, so you must supply a title that will route the mailing to the desired person.

4. When you finish defining the code and suppression/replacement options as needed, a Message screen will prompt you to

```
Align printer and press enter to continue
```

Make sure your printer is on-line before pressing **<ENTER>**. Otherwise you will get an error message. Retry with your printer on-line.

Print Selected Records

This option from the Print Menu allows you to select specific records from the database and assemble a custom list. Remember, the mailing lists you create are virtual; that is, they only exist for output sake (although you can output to an ASCII file, thereby explicitly saving the extracted list for later use). Take the following steps to assemble a virtual mailing list:

1. When you press **2**, a Report Criteria Input screen will be displayed. Notice that the screen is identical to the input screen you used to input and edit records, with the exception that the name field is not present, the zip code field is divided in two, and a number of code selection fields are available on the bottom of the screen (under the Include/Exclude labels).

The principle is the same as that used to scan for records (see above), except that you can enter a search criteria in any highlighted field on the screen. When you enter selections in each field of the record, you are actually instructing the program as to which records you would like to include in a particular mailing list. If you leave a field blank, that indicates you want to include all records.

For example, if you leave the Title, Department, Company, and City fields blank, enter OH for state, and leave the Zip and Country fields blank, you are selecting records that have Ohio in the state field and anything else in the remaining fields. You could further refine the mailing by indicating a range of zip codes (which is why the field is split into two), or certain titles, such as President or Manager. When you have entered the code criteria (see below), you will have assembled a custom mailing list comprised of selected records from your database.

ATTRIBUTE CODES

Attribute codes allow you to add people with particular demographic characteristics, job titles, purchasing or giving habits, or whatever designations you are using. The three code fields below the Include label are linked by AND, while those below the Exclude label are linked by OR. That means that if you fill in all three Attribute code fields, a record must have *all* three attributes to be included in the list you are assembling. If you filled in all three fields under the EXCLUDE label, any single attribute will preclude it from being assembled into the list.

Let's say that you want to include attribute codes 55K and VPM, but you want to exclude attribute codes 002 or 004 (perhaps 002 and 004 stand for certain industrial sectors). To be part of the list, the record must have 55K *and* VPM in its attribute field. But it would be disqualified from the list if it had either 002 *or* 004 in the attribute field.

USAGE CODES

These codes are used to select records based on their inclusion in previous mailing lists. Remember that the Usage codes are actually list codes that you specified when you created lists earlier. When you requested the program to Update records (see above), the list code was inserted into the usage field. The usage field can maintain the codes for the last five lists for which the record was updated.

For instance, if you had recently included Mr. Smith's record in a list that you called ABCD, and you had requested that the records be Updated, the record would contain the usage code ABCD in the Usage code Field (assuming that you had not updated that record five times since creating the ABCD list and pushed ABCD out of the record). Now you can either include or exclude Mr. Smith from a new list compilation based on his ABCD usage code. This is a powerful feature that allows you to build new lists based on previous usage history.

2. After you have input the desired selection criteria and begun the search, the program will display the Sort Order Selection Menu described above. Select the order by which you want records to be printed. The program will then look for records that match the criteria you input, and create a report from them. If no records are located, the program displays the message

```
No records meet your criteria.
Press any key to continue
```

3. If any records match your criteria, the program will display the Criteria Search Results screen, which indicates how many records met your criteria. The Criteria Search Results

screen gives you the following options, in addition to pressing **ESC** to return to the Main Menu:

***Press* P** *to print.* Use this option if you wish to print out the selected records. You will be presented with the Report Selection Menu. The menu will indicate how many records are to be printed, along with the criteria you used to select them. The report formats are the same as those used to print the entire database (see above for a description). Note that when reports are printed out after a criteria search, the criteria used will be indicated at the top of the page.

***Press* S** *to display on screen.* Before you print a report, you may want to view the mailing list records first to make sure you have retrieved the correct one(s). Or, you may just wish to review the selected records on the screen. This option allows you to do either. When you press S, the screen will display the complete record for the first record that met your search criteria, in Scanning Screen format. If more than one record was found, you can page forward and backward through the selected records by using **F** (forward) and **B** (backward). The principle is the same as that used in the editing process.

After you are finished examining the selected records, press **0** to return to the Report Selection Menu. You can then print the selected records, or return to the Main Menu by pressing **0**.

Using Utilities

The Mailing List Management Program includes four housekeeping functions for maintaining the database. These are accessed from the Utilities Menu, which you used earlier to set up the program. The Utilities Menu is accessed by selecting Option #4 from the Main Menu. The options are described below.

Reindex. Occasionally, you may find that the search routines are not operating correctly. The most probable cause for this is a damaged index. This usually results from illegally exiting the program (see Exiting, below). If this should occur, you must reindex the files by selecting Option #1 from the Utilities Menu. The reindexing option will take a variable period of time, depending on the number of records in the file and the type of computer you are using.

Pack. Packing is the final stage used to delete marked records (refer to Editing/Viewing/Deleting Records, above). Unlike marking a record, though, packing is an irreversible action; once a mailing list record is packed, it no longer exists. After selecting the pack option, the program will display how many records will be packed, and you will be asked to confirm your choice with a **Y** plus an **<ENTER>**. The packing process can take several minutes or longer, since it must update all indexes.

Delete usage codes. You may occasionally wish to purge usage codes from the entire database to permit a clean start for all records. Select this option only if you really want to purge them all. You will be asked to confirm your choice before the purging actually takes place.

If you want to purge all usage codes from selected records, you can do so by creating a report list of the records to be cleaned, updating them five successive times with a blank list code. This will have the effect of pushing all existing codes out of the record.

System setup. The Mailing List Management Program uses the dBXL To Go basic setup options described in Chapter 1.

Note: If you want to delete all records and start with a clean database, you can either recopy the .dbf files from your distribution diskette or use the dBXL Zap command to erase all records. **Zap** simultaneously deletes and packs all records in your database. To use **Zap**, make current the directory in which you keep your Mailing List Management Program files. Start dBXL, and then at the prompt type:

```
use mail
```

Next, type:

```
zap
```

dBXL will ask you to confirm the action with a **Y** or **N**. When you select **Y**, all records will be deleted and packed from your database. After zapping, you must reindex to ensure that your indexes correspond to the program.

> **CAUTION**: Zap is an irrevocable command; there is no way to recover a zapped file. Therefore, back up your data before zapping it!

Exiting

It is vitally important that you properly exit from the Mailing List Management Program. Failure to do so may cause file or index damage. While it is often possible to remedy the situation by reindexing, the damage may be permanent, in which case you must start over again by copying the files from your working diskette and re-entering your data, or restoring your database from your most recent backup copy. Given the needless waste of time and the aggravation in reconstructing a database, *always exit by pressing* **0** *in the menu you are working with until you reach the Main Menu.* Pressing **0** at the Main Menu will close all database files and return you to a Sign-Off screen, which asks you if you wish to leave the program. Entering **Y** returns you to DOS, and entering **N** returns you to the Main Menu. (Note: If you are running an uncompiled program, pressing **X** will return you to the dBXL prompt.)

7 Manual For Time Billing Program

Features

- Menu driven.
- Password protection.
- Comprehensive system for tracking and billing professional time.
- Easy to use electronic time sheets.
- Auto lookup of client information speeds data entry.
- Powerful invoice generator allows you to create, view, and print invoices for any time period.
- Accepts 12-hour or 24-hour time scale.
- Allows for easy analysis of time allocation by client.
- Accounts receivable report shows aging for all or selected clients.

Contents

Introduction

The Time Billing Program is designed for professional firms that bill on an hourly basis. It enables you to input billable hours and billing rates for various members of the firm, and to generate reports that compute the total time your firm spent on various client projects. You can also use the program to create client invoices and to track them through the billing cycle.

The program consists of five separate databases that are linked together to generate reports and invoices. At any time, you can total the time that each employee has spent working for a given client to date. This provides a valuable tool for ensuring that clients are billed on a timely basis. It also serves as a reminder when certain benchmarks or dollar limits have been met. Invoices can also be generated at any time.

Before using the program, read through this manual and familiarize yourself with all the input, report, and utility functions. You may want to set up a practice time billing system, using two or three time sheets to review the functions of the program. Also, create a backup disk for your database files (Timebill.dbf, Timeclnt.dbf, Timeempl.dbf, Timeproj.dbf, and Timetask.dbf). there's no need to back up your program (.prg), format (.fmt), or report (.frm) files. you can always recopy them from your working diskette. You don't have to back up your index files either, since your program creates them if they aren't found in the directory.

At a minimum, back up your .dbf files each time you add or edit records; the few minutes that the procedure requires will more than offset the time you would need to spend if the entire database had to be recreated. Remember, no hardware system is infallible, and it's better to be safe than sorry!

Finally, if you are an experienced dBXL user and wish to modify the program, refer to the Technical Appendix charts and tables. You will find a program tree that lists the calling program hierarchy, a table that describes each index file, and a list of files required to run the program.

Data Entry Keys

After you have input data, provided that you haven't pressed **<ENTER>**, you may use the Backspace key to erase your entry, or the cursor arrows and Delete/Insert keys to modify your entry. When you do press **<ENTER>**, the cursor will move to the next data input field. If you need to return to a previous entry, use the up cursor key to move the cursor to the desired field. Enter your changes and press **<ENTER>** to move on through the input screen. Note that any errors made during data entry can also be corrected later by means of the Edit option, described below.

Installing and Setting up the Program

Before you begin using the Time Billing Program, you will have to install and set it up. General instructions for installation and setup are contained in Chapter 1.

Starting the Program

The easiest way to start the Time Billing Program is to create a batch file. You can also start the program manually by typing

```
do time
```

after starting dBXL (see Chapter 1 for specifics of both startup techniques).

Regardless of how you begin the Time Billing Program, you will first see the dBXL copyright and license notice.The screen will display the message "Creating indexes, please wait." This process may require a few seconds, but only occurs the first time you run the program after installation. The Time Billing Program Main Menu then will appear.

Entering Time Data

Data is entered into Time Sheet Input screens, much as you would create a manual time sheet with pen and paper. Before you can enter data into a time sheet, however, you must prepare various support files, which contain information about your clients, the employees in your firm, your projects, and the specific tasks performed on those projects. Once you have entered the basic information into the support files, the program will automatically insert it into the appropriate field on each time sheet you create. For example, if you have indicated that John Smith's billing rate is $125 per hour, when John Smith is entered into a time sheet, the program will insert 125 into the rate field. If client A-1000 is the number for The ABC Company, when you enter A-1000 in the client number field, the program will insert The ABC Company and all address data into the address fields.

Four support files are necessary to fill out a time sheet. To create them (or edit or add to them later), select Option #2 from the Main Menu, Create Support Files. The Support File Menu will then be displayed. Use the following steps to fill out the input screens.

Support Files

CREATING A CLIENT SUPPORT FILE

Select Option #1 from the Support Menu, and the program will display the Client Input screen, which allows you to put in basic demographic data about the client you will be billing:

1. Number: Even if you do not use client numbers, you must assign them to use this program. The number can be any combination of six alphabetic or numeric characters.

2. Name: Input the name of the person to whom the invoice will be sent. Enter the last name first. Enter the appropriate information in each of the following fields, pressing **<ENTER>** when you are finished.
3. Title:
4. Company:
5. Street:
6. City:
7. State:
8. Zip:

To save the information into the database, press **<ENTER>** after entering the zip code. You can also save the data at any time by pressing **CTRL-END**. If you do not want to save your entries, press **ESC**.

CREATE AN EMPLOYEE RECORD

Basic information about your firm's employees can be entered into a support file by selecting Option #2 of the Support File Menu, which displays the Employee Input screen. Fill out the following fields, and then use **CTRL-END** or **<ENTER>** on the last field (Hourly Rate) to save the data into the support file. Repeat the process for each employee.

1. Number: Even if you do not presently use employee numbers, you must assign them to use the Time Billing Program. The number can be a mix of alphabetic and numeric characters.

2. First Name/Last Name:

3. Department: (optional)

4. Hourly Rate: Do not enter a dollar sign. If the rate is in whole dollars, just press **<ENTER>**. dBXL will insert .00 for you.

Save by pressing **CTRL-END**, or press **ESC** to abandon the screen without saving your entries.

PROJECT SUPPORT FILE

The project support file simply assigns a number and name to a project. Select Option #3 from the Support File Menu, and fill out the two fields on the Project Input screen. Create a new record for each project.

1. Number: You must assign a project number for the program to work. The number can be any combination of alphanumeric characters.

2. Project: This field is for a project name, designation, or code.

As above, save by pressing **CTRL-END**, or press **ESC** to abandon the screen without saving your entries.

TASK SUPPORT FILE

Select Option #4 from the Support File Menu to display the Task Input screen. Enter a code for the specific kind of task that is performed on a given project (e.g., writing, programming, general consulting, research, deposition, etc.). If more than one task is performed for a project, create additional task code records. The Task Input screen consists of two fields.

1. Number: You must have a task number for the program to work; enter any combination of alphanumeric characters.

2. Task: Assign a task name for your reference.

Save your entries by pressing **CTRL-END** or press **ESC** to abandon the screen without saving your entries.

Once you have completed support files for your existing clients and tasks, you are ready to begin filling out time sheets. Whenever you acquire a new client or project, or add a new task, be sure that you create a support file for them before filling out a time sheet. Hint: Use the report generator (see below) to create printouts of all your support files. Keep the printouts by the computer, so everyone entering time sheet data will use the same codes.

Filling Out Time Sheets

When you select Option #1, Create Time Sheets, from the Main Menu, a blank Time Sheet Input screen will be displayed. The time sheet consists of three major sections:

Employee data. Provides fields for key employee information, such as number and rate.

Client/project/task information. Cross-references coding information previously entered into support files. Also displays time information for each task.

Time bill summary. Displays summary information for up to 10 time record entries. When the tenth record is completed, the data is added to a master file, and a new time sheet is displayed. (Details of this mechanism are explained below, under Processing Time Records.)

EMPLOYEE DATA SECTION

The Time Billing program uses a blank employee number, client number, project number, or task number to designate your decision to exit the Time Sheet input process. You can exit at any time by leaving one of these fields blank and pressing **<ENTER>** or **ESC**. If you have already entered data into a field and want to exit, you must first remove the data with the space bar or Backspace key before pressing **<ENTER>** or **ESC**.

Each time you press **<ENTER>**, the cursor will move through the following sequence of fields:

Employee. Enter one of the employee numbers you entered into the employee support files. If the number is not in a support file, the program will display this message at the bottom of the time sheet:

```
EMPLOYEE NOT FOUND
```

At that point, you have two options. Either press **<ENTER>** and re-enter the correct number, or exit the time sheet and create the number in the employee support file. To exit the program, overwrite whatever you typed by pressing the space bar so the field is blank, and then press **<ENTER>**. The Main Menu will be displayed, after which you can create a new support record.

If the employee number is correct, the employee's name will be displayed in the top of the time sheet, along with the employee's hourly billing rate and the employee's department.

CLIENT/TASK DATA SECTION

Client. Enter the client code. If the code is not valid, the program will inform you that the code is not on file. Re-enter the code, or blank out your entry by overwriting it with the space bar and press **<ENTER>** to redisplay the Main Menu.

Project. Enter the project code. The process described in Client is used if you enter an incorrect code.

Task. Input the appropriate task code; same procedure as Client and Project for incorrect entries.

Date. The date defaults to the current system date. Accept it by pressing **<ENTER>**, or use the cursor keys to edit it.

Start. Enter the time started. The field in front of the colon is for hours, the field after for minutes. You must press **<ENTER>** to input each field. Note: If you worked past midnight on a project, you must split the time record into two entries, the second beginning at 00:01 on the following date. You can use either a 12- or 24-hour time designation, although the 24-hour will provide the least ambiguous records.

Stop. Input the time that the employee completed the task.

Time. This field can be used in one of two ways. If you leave it blank, the elapsed time will be computed when the record is complete. If you enter a value, whatever you enter will supercede the calculation. This is helpful when you want to bill a client for more or less time than has actually elapsed. You might, for example, have worked for an hour, but received a 15-minute phone call unrelated to the client work, and wish to bill the client for 45 minutes rather than an hour. This is easier than creating two records, one for pre-phone call and one for post-phone call. Alternately, another person might have contributed to the project, and you may want to include that person's contribution without creating an additional record.

In any case, when you press **<ENTER>** in the minutes field, the cursor will move to the next field, Rate. When you press **<ENTER>** in the Rate field, the elapsed time will be calculated, unless you have previously overwritten it with a specific time value.

Rate. The rate from the appropriate employee support file record will be automatically inserted into this field. If you wish, you may edit the rate by overwriting it with a new one. As soon as you press **<ENTER>**, the total amount (hours times rate) will be calculated and displayed in the Fee field.

Fee. Press **<ENTER>** to accept the calculated amount, or overwrite it by entering a new amount and pressing **<ENTER>**. When you do so, the bottom of the screen will display the message

```
ENTRY CONFIRMATION--PROCESS (Y/N) ?
```

If you enter **Y**, the entire record as input will be appended to a temporary file, and will then appear on Line 1 of the Time Bill Summary section. The cursor will then return to the Employee field, so you can enter the employee's next task.

If you enter N, the program assumes that you want to edit one of the fields, and the record will not be appended to the temporary file. The cursor will return to the Employee field. You can press **<ENTER>** to advance the cursor to any of the fields and edit them with the Backspace or Delete keys. You can, in fact, recreate the entire record if you wish. If you want to quit the entry process altogether, use the space bar to clean out any data in the Client, Project, Employee, or Task fields, and press **<ENTER>** or **ESC**.

Processing Time Records

After adding your tenth record to the Time Billing Summary section or escaping from the input process using the blank field technique described above, the screen will display the following message:

```
PROCESS DATA (Y/N)
```

If you enter **Y**, the batch of up to 10 records will be appended to the master file. You may then fill out another time sheet. Note that the employee, client, project, and task codes from the previous time sheet will be maintained on the screen in their appropriate fields, so you can continue adding data. You can edit any of the fields by overwriting them with new data.

If you select **N**, at the Process Data prompt, the time entry records will not be appended to the master file. CAUTION: By selecting **N**, you will lose all time record entries for that batch (up to the 10 records displayed on the screen), and will have to re-input them!!

Editing/Viewing/Deleting Records

The Scan Function

To recall a previously created time sheet or support file record, select the Edit/Delete Records option from the Main Menu (Option #3). Choose the type of record(s) you would like to locate through the program's scan function.

Scanning is used to search for a record or group of records, and then to display them on the screen. It is useful for two purposes. First, it will enable you to pinpoint a specific record for viewing, editing, or deleting, as explained below. Second, you can locate a group of records and display them one by one for editing or deletion.

One way to think of the second scan function is to imagine the records on a track. When you scan for, say, all time sheets for Client A-1000, the program will find the first record that has A-1000 in the Client field. It will then display that record in Scanning format (see below). You can view the records one after another, forward and backward (by pressing **F** and **B**; see editing options, below). The records will appear alphabetically or numerically in the order determined by the criteria you selected. If you enter a blank scan criteria and press **<ENTER>** or **ESC**, the program will display the first record in the database, according to the criteria you selected.

Note: You can use contractions of the name you are seeking and the program will find the first record matching the contractions. For example, if you only enter C for a scan by name, the program will display the first record starting with the letter C.

Scanning Time Sheets

1. If you select Option #1 from the Edit/Delete Menu, the Scan Selection Menu will be displayed, offering you five different methods for scanning time sheets: invoice, client, employee, project, and task numbers.

2. When you select any of the options from the Time Sheet Scan Selection Menu, the program will display an input screen in which you can enter a specific request.

    For example, when you select Option #5, Scan Records by Task Number, the Scanning Criteria Input screen appears. If you enter 501, the program will locate all time sheets in which 501 appears in the Task field. The records will be organized by task number. The same procedure is used for the other scan criteria options available from the menu. Once the records are located, you can view, modify, or delete them using the options described below.

Support Files

The scan function can be used to locate a specific record in your support files.

1. When the Edit/Delete Menu is displayed, you will have two options for locating records in the support file. Option #2 allows you to scan a support file by name (e.g., client name, employee name, etc.), while Option #3 is used to scan by number (client number, employee number or code, etc.).

    (Suggestion: Use the first letter of the client's name followed by a number, such as A-1000 for ABC Corp.)

2. When you select either option, the program displays the Edit/Delete Selection Menu. Select the desired scan criteria, and an input screen will allow you to enter your scan criteria. Once you have found the record you are seeking, use the standard edit/delete functions described below.

3. If no time sheets or support file records in the database match the name or word entered in the scan input screen, the program will display the following message:

    ```
    No records meet your criteria.
    Press any key to continue
    ```

4. If any records do match the word(s) you entered, the record(s) you are seeking will be displayed in Scanning screen format. You can then use the following functions to view, edit, or delete the records.

F = Forward, B = Backward. Each time your press **F**, you will browse forward from one record to another. To move backward through the file, press **B**. The program will move backward one record each time the **B** key is pressed. If you try to scan past the end of the file (the record most recently input), or the beginning of the file (the first record entered), the program will beep and remain on the last, or first, record.

E =Edit. Once you have located a record that you would like to alter, select **E** and the program will switch to full screen edit mode. Each field will be highlighted on the screen, just as it was during initial data entry. You can move from highlighted field to highlighted field by using the cursor, or by pressing **<ENTER>**. Each time you press **<ENTER>**, the cursor will advance one field. Make your changes in a field using the Backspace, Insert, and Delete keys. The editing process is ended by pressing **CTRL-END** in any field, or by pressing **<ENTER>** in the last field. Either action will save the information to disk. You can exit without saving the changes to disk by pressing the **ESC** key.

D=Delete. Deletion with the Time Billing Program is a two-step process. First, press **D** to mark the record for deletion. MARKED FOR DELETION will appear above the menu options. Although a record is marked for deletion, it is not actually removed from the database until you use the Pack function, which is accessed from the Utilities Menu (see below). Records may remain in the marked state indefinitely. Even when you exit the program and return at a later date, records slated for deletion will still be marked.

U = Undelete. If you decide that you do not want to delete a marked record and you haven't used the Pack function yet, you can unmark the record by selecting the **U** option. The MARKED FOR DELETION message will then be removed from the record.

0=Exit. When you select the **0** option, the program will return to the Main Menu.

Generating Reports

The Time Billing Program allows you to output your time sheets and support files records in several different report formats. All of the reports will line up properly on 8.5 x ll-inch paper using condensed (15 characters per inch) type. If you specified in the setup phase that you have two printers, reports will be automatically output to the printer attached to LPTl:, while invoices will be printed on LPT2:.

Invoices are treated as a separate function, and are created by selecting Option #5 from the Main Menu. To begin the report generation process, select Option #4 from the Main Menu. The Print Menu will then be displayed, offering you the following choices:

1. Print time sheets.
2. Print support files.
3. Print accounts receivable report.

The steps for outputting the three types of reports follow.

Print Time Sheets

Determine a sort order. After choosing Option #l from the Print Menu, the Sort Order Selection Menu will be displayed. This menu allows you to choose the numerical order in which records will be printed on the reports. For example, if you choose Option #l (Client), the records will be printed in numerical sequence by client.

Indicate the Date and Status Criteria. After you choose a sort order, the program will display a Print Criteria Input Screen.

1. Enter the starting and ending service dates for the time sheets you wish to print.

2. Enter payment status of time sheets you wish to print: All, OPEN (unpaid), or PAID.

3. Enter the billing status: Y for time sheets that have been billed, N for time sheets that have not been billed. Entering a blank selects both billed and unbilled time records.

4. When you press **<ENTER>** after inputting the billing status, the program will search for records that match your criteria. If you wish to abort the process, press **ESC**. If no records match the search criteria, the following message will be displayed:

   ```
   No records meet your criteria
   Press any key to continue
   ```

5. If any records do match your criteria, the program will display a Criteria Search Results screen, which indicates the number of records that met the criteria. Press **P** to display the Report Selection Menu, or **ESC** to abort the process and return to the Main Menu.

Choose a report. The Report Selection Menu offers you two different types of time sheet reports:

1. Detailed Report. Includes the Record Number; the Invoice Number and Invoice Date; the Employee, Client, Project, and Task numbers; the Service Date; Start and Stop time and Elapsed Time; and the Fee. The report also indicates the payment status. It prints one line per time sheet.

2. Summary Report. Breaks out the fee by time sheet, with no line item details.

Once you have selected the type of report you want to print, a Message screen will prompt you to:

```
align printer and press enter to continue.
```

Make sure your printer is on-line before pressing **<ENTER>**. Otherwise you will get an error message. Retry with your printer on-line.

Print Support File Reports

Choose the report type. When you select Option #2 from the Print Menu, the program will display the Print Order Selection Menu, which offers you two types of support file reports.

1. Support file report by name. Outputs all data on each support record, organized by the (client, project, employee, task) name input on each record.

2. Support file report by number. Same as above, but organizes reports by number (employee, client, project, task).

Select the support file you wish to print. Once you select a report type, the program will display the Support File Report Selection Menu. The menu offers you options for printing client, employee, project, or task records. Once you make your selection, the program will prompt you to align the printer. If the printer is on-line, your report will be generated to LPT1:. If not, the error message described above will be displayed.

Print Accounts Receivable Report

Enter the print criteria. When you select Option #3 from the Print Menu, the program will display the A/R Criteria Screen. If you want an A/R Report that ages all open invoices, enter a blank by pressing **<ENTER>**. If you want to generate an aged receivable report for a special client, enter the client code.

Once you've made your selection, the program will ask whether you wish to print the report. Pressing **Y** will output the report to the printer attached to LPT1:. Pressing **N** outputs the report to your screen.

Generating Invoices

The Time Billing Program is equipped with a powerful invoice generator that allows you to sweep any time period and assemble invoices for billable time. You can view invoices before printing them, and blow up an invoice to examine the detail line items. To begin the invoice generation process, select Option #5 from the Main Menu. The Invoice Processing Menu will then appear. The following discussion explains how to use each option.

Assemble Invoices. When you select this option from the Invoice Processing Menu, the program will display an Invoicing Criteria Input screen that allows you to set the date range for which you would like billable time assembled into invoices. Enter the starting and ending dates for the range, and the program will look through all the master time records not yet billed and organize them by client. A message will appear at the bottom of the screen:

```
PROCESS INVOICING (Y/N) ?
```

If you press **Y**, a results screen will be displayed, showing you how many line items (time entry records) were found for that date range, and how many clients will be billed for those entries. (Pressing **N** at the prompt will return you to the input screen.) If no line items were found for the time period you specified, the program will display the message:

```
No records meet your criteria.
Press any key to continue
```

Once you press a key, you will return to the Invoice Processing Menu.

After individual time records are assembled into an invoice, they are permanently associated with that invoice unless you manually edit the invoice number by means of the edit option described above. Be certain that you want to assemble the invoices for the time period entered before proceeding with invoice assembly.

View invoices. After you have assembled a batch of invoices, you can scan them, just as you scanned time sheets and support file records above. In addition to viewing the total amounts and line items, you can get an exploded view of each invoice and scroll through the line items that comprise the bill.

1. The viewing process begins when you select Option #2 from the Invoice Processing Menu. This will invoke the Invoice Scanning Criteria screen.

2. Select the index by which you would like to scan the invoices, and an input screen will prompt you to enter a client name, client number, or invoice number, depending on which scan criteria you selected. The search will begin after you press **<ENTER>**. Press **ESC** if you wish to start with the first invoice based on the selected criteria.

3. If no records meet your scan criteria, the program will display the standard noncriteria match, and prompt you to press a key to continue. The Invoice Processing Menu will then be redisplayed.

4. If any records do match your scan criteria, the invoices will be displayed according to the scan criteria you selected. An invoice gives the client's name and address, the invoice number, date, amount, and status. You can now use any of the options shown at the bottom of the Invoice Scanning Screen, which include the following functions. You can exit from view mode at any time by pressing **ESC**, which will return you to the Invoice Processing Menu.

Note: Because of the complexity of the searching routines, some functions may take a few seconds longer than you would normally expect, depending on the type of computer you are using. If you don't get an instant response after selecting an option, be patient—do not press **<ENTER>** in an effort to confirm your choice. The **<ENTER>** will only catch up later and possibly cause an unexpected display or action.

F=Forward, B=Backward. Press **F** to page forward through the invoices, and **B** to page backward. The program will beep when you back up to the end of the file or go forward to the beginning of the file. You can print or view the detail listings of each invoice by using the **P** and **V** options, or update the status by pressing **$**, as described below.

P = Print. If you wish to print the invoice, press **P**. Make sure that your printer is on-line. Remember, if you indicated that you have two printers, the invoices will automatically print to LPT2:.

V=View. This option enables you to get an exploded view of an invoice and examine each line item. When you press **V**, the screen will display a maximum of five time record entries. You can scroll the entries by pressing **F** or **B**. If there are no more line entries to view and you try to scroll forward or backward, the program will beep. The invoice total will show on the bottom right corner of the screen.

$=Paid. When an invoice has been paid, you should update the status by pressing the **$** sign. This will mark the invoice and adjust your report totals accordingly.

Print invoices. Whereas the print option described above is useful for outputting a small number of selected invoices, this option is used to output a range of invoices. (They will automatically be printed on LPT2: if you indicated two printers during setup.)

1. When you select Option #3 from the Invoice Processing Menu, the Invoice Printing Criteria Input Screen will be displayed. Enter the starting and ending invoice dates and numbers. You can enter any or all criteria.

2. If no invoices match the date and number criteria you input, the program will indicate that no records were found, and tell you to press any key to continue.

3. If any records do match the date and numbering criteria, a message screen will indicate how many line items will be printed, and how many clients will be invoiced. Press **Y** if you wish to continue, and **ESC** if you wish to abort the printing process and return to the Invoice Processing Menu. If you proceed with the printing, the program will prompt you to align the paper and press enter. Make sure your printer is on-line. After the invoices are printed, the Invoice Processing Menu will be redisplayed.

Using Utilities

The Time Billing Program includes three housekeeping utility functions for maintaining the database. These are accessed from the Utilities Menu, which you used earlier to set up the program. The Utilities Menu is accessed by selecting Option #6 from the Main Menu. The utility options are described below.

Reindex. Occasionally, you may find that the search routines are not operating correctly. The most probable cause for this is a damaged index. This usually results from illegally exiting the program (see below for the proper exit routine). If this should occur, you must reindex the files by selecting Option # 1 from the Utilities Menu. The reindexing option will take a variable period of time depending on the number of records in the file. The reindexing process is initiated as soon as you select Option #1 from the Utilities Menu.

Pack. Packing is the final stage used to delete marked records (refer to Editing/Viewing/Deleting Records, above). Unlike marking a record, though, packing is irreversible; once a record is packed, it no longer exists. After selecting the pack option, the program will display how many records will be packed, and you will be asked to confirm your choice with a **Y** plus **<ENTER>**. The packing process can take several minutes or longer, since it must update all indexes.

System setup. In addition to the basic setup options described in Chapter 1, the Time Billing Program uses the following special setup options.

1. Number of Printers. The program allows you to run two different printers, one for invoices, the other for statements. If you indicate that you have two printers, the system will automatically output invoices to LPT2:, and statements and reports to LPTl:. If you specify one printer, the program will direct all output to LPT1: .

2. Top Spacing for Invoice. If you choose to print invoices on your own letterhead, you must indicate how far down the page the printing should begin so that it will not overwrite your name or address. Enter the appropriate number of lines in the space provided. If you wish to create a letterhead using the Header Text option (see below), you must still indicate where the body of the invoice is to be printed by indicating the desired top spacing. This is especially important if you wish to modify the invoice text at some future time. The maximum Top Spacing will depend on the length of the text you use and the available lines of print per page on your printer.

3. Header Text. This option allows you to print a letterhead of your own choosing. You can enter up to five lines, with a maximum of 60 characters each. Type in each line exactly as you wish it to appear on your invoices. You can enter a single- or double-dashed line to separate the header from the body of the invoice. If you enter a header text, you must ensure that the top spacing is set at 7 (lines) or greater. Otherwise, the text will be overwritten by the body of the invoice. Note: This setup option does not automatically center text, as the Company/User option does. Position your entries exactly as you would like them to

appear in print. When you finish entering your header and press **<ENTER>**, your setup choices will be saved and the Main Menu will be redisplayed.

Note: If you want to delete all records and start with a clean database, you can either recopy the .dbf files from your distribution diskette or use the dBXL Zap command to erase all records. Zap simultaneously deletes and packs all records in your database. To use Zap, make current the directory in which you keep your Time Billing Program files. Start dBXL, and at the prompt type:

```
use timebill
```

Next, type:

```
zap
```

dBXL will ask you to confirm the action with a **Y** or **N**. When you select **Y**, all records will be erased and deleted from the timebill database. Repeat the Zap procedure with the remaining databases: timeclnt, timeempl, timeproj, and timetask. After using the Zap command, you must reindex to ensure that your indexes correspond to the program.

> **CAUTION**: Zap is an irrevocable command; there is no way to recover a zapped file. Therefore, back up your data before zapping it!

Exiting

It is vitally important that you properly exit from the Time Billing Program. Failure to do so may cause file or index damage. While it is often possible to remedy the situation by reindexing, the damage may be permanent, in which case you must start over by copying the files from your working diskette and re-entering your data, or restoring your database from your most recent backup copy. Given the needless waste of time and the aggravation in reconstructing a database, always exit by pressing **0** in the menu you are working with until you reach the Main Menu. Pressing **0** at the Main Menu will close all database files and return you to a Sign-Off screen that asks you if you wish to leave the program. Entering **Y** returns you to DOS; entering **N** returns you to the Main Menu. Note: If you are running an uncompiled program, pressing **X** will return you to the dBXL prompt.

8 Manual For Travel Expense Reporting Program

Features

- Menu driven.
- Password protection.
- Complete system for tracking business travel expenses.
- Enables you to track expenses by traveler, client, department, and budget center.
- Comprehensive reporting system.
- Sorts travel expense reports by employee, client, department, or budget center.
- Choice of detail or summary reports.

Contents

Introduction

The Travel Expense Reporting Program makes it easy to keep track of travel expenses incurred by various members of your firm on behalf of clients. Once information is logged into the database, you can generate reports that break out the traveler's total expenses as well as the expenses that can be billed to various clients. You can also create reports that link travel expenses to departments and budget centers.

The program is set up so that you enter one record per trip or day. Fields are provided for the most common expense categories (e.g., transportation means, meals, entertainment, etc.). While it is still useful to provide travelers in your firm with a form that they can fill out and later submit for data entry, the program can provide invaluable information for analyzing travel expenses and ensuring that clients are invoiced for all billable expenses.

Before using the program, read through this manual and familiarize yourself with all the input, report, and utility functions. You may want to set up a practice expense management system, using two or three expense records to review the functions of the program. Also, create a backup disk for your database file (Travel.dbf). There's no need to back up your program (.prg), format (.fmt), or report (.frm) files. You can always recopy them from your working diskette. You don't have to back up your index files either, since your program creates them if they aren't found in the directory.

At a minimum, back up your .dbf files each time you add or edit records; the few minutes that the procedure requires will more than offset the time you would need to spend if the entire database had to be recreated. Remember, *no* hardware system is infallible, and it's better to be safe than sorry!

Finally, if you are an experienced dBXL user and wish to modify the program, refer to the Technical Appendix charts and tables. You will find a program tree that lists the calling program hierarchy, a table that describes each index file, and a list of files required to run the program.

Data Entry Keys

After you have input data, you may use the Backspace key to erase your entry (provided that you haven't pressed **<ENTER>**). Alternately, you can use the cursor and Delete/Insert keys to modify your entry. When you do press **<ENTER>**, the cursor will move to the next data input field. If you need to return to a previous entry, use the up cursor key to move the cursor to the desired field. Enter your changes and press **<ENTER>** to move on through the input screen. Note that any errors made during data entry can also be corrected later by means of the Edit option.

Installing and Setting up the Program

Before you begin using the Travel Expense Reporting Program, you will have to install and set it up. General instructions for installation and setup are contained in Chapter l.

Starting the Program

The easiest way to start the Travel Expense Program is to create a batch file. You can also start the program manually by typing

```
do travel
```

after starting dBXL (see Chapter 1 for specifics of both startup techniques).

Regardless of how you begin the Travel Expense Reportign Program, you will first see the dBXL copyright and license notice. The screen will display the message "Creating indexes, please wait." This process may require a few seconds, but only occurs the first time you run the program after installation. The Travel Expense Program Main Menu will then appear.

Entering Travel Expense Records

All information is entered through the Travel Expense Input Screen, which is called up by selecting Option #1, Add Records, from the Main Menu. The Travel Expense Input Screen consists of two sections:

Excursion data section. Provides fields for information about traveler, destination, and trip accounting.

Expense section. Contains fields for basic travel expense categories. Each category is further broken down into charges paid by the company, and charges paid out-of-pocket by the traveler (labeled Personal).

Excursion Data Section

When the Travel Expense Input screen is displayed, the cursor will move through the following sequence of fields each time you press <ENTER>:

Traveler. Enter the traveler's name, initials, or ID code. It is very important that you enter data in this field consistently. dBXL treats punctuation marks and spaces as valid characters, so that records with P.G.R. in the Traveler field will not be grouped together and subtotaled with records that have PGR (no periods) in the Traveler field. Make sure everyone who enters data is aware of the system you devise for coding or abbreviating names.

Client. Enter the client on behalf of whom the travel expenses were incurred. The same consistency issues described above apply to this field. You are probably best off assigning client codes rather than using names, since codes are less likely to be entered inconsistently. If you use client codes, we recommend keeping a list of them by the computer for all operators to use.

Destination. Use words or abbreviations to describe the itinerary. This field is not sorted, so consistency is only a matter of aesthetics on reports.

Date. Enter the travel date.

Department. If the travel is to be charged to a certain department within your company, enter the name or code. Consistency is important with this field, since it is used for subtotaling and sorting. A coding system might therefore be more useful than department names.

Budget. If relevant, enter the budget center to which the department is related. This field is used for subtotaling and sorting, so consistency issues are again relevant.

Expense Section

This part of the screen is divided into basic expense categories. Each category has a field labeled Company, and a field labeled Personal. If the expense was either prepaid by the company, or paid with a company credit card, enter it in the Company field. If the traveler paid for it out-of-pocket, enter it in the Personal field. Each time you press <ENTER>, the cursor will move through the following sequence of expense category fields:

1. L.D. Travel:
2. Local Travel:
3. Lodging:
4. Entertainment:
5. Breakfast:
6. Lunch:
7. Dinner:
8. Miscellaneous:

Notice that the last field in the Expense Record Input screen is the Total field. This field is calculated by the program once you have entered data in all the relevant preceding fields. The calculated total appears on the Edit screen (see below) and on all reports.

Adding Another Expense Record

When you press <ENTER> while the cursor is in the Miscellaneous/Personal field, or press **CTRL-END** elsewhere during data input, the record will be included in the database. A prompt at the bottom of the screen will then ask if you want to add another record. To accept the default **Y** and continue adding records, press <ENTER>. If you enter **N**, the program will return to the Main Menu. Note: You must, at a minimum, enter a traveler's name or a client's name for a record to be complete and added to the database.

Editing/Viewing/Deleting Records

The Scan Function

To recall a previously created travel expense record, select Edit /Delete Records from the Main Menu (Option #2), and select a criteria by which you will scan for records in the database (the choices are employee, client, department,or budget).

Scanning searches for a record or group of records, and then displays them on the screen. It is useful for two purposes. First, it will enable you to pinpoint a specific record for viewing, editing, or deleting, as explained below. Second, you can locate a group of records, after which you can display them one by one for editing or deletion.

One way to think of the second scan function is to imagine the records on a track. When you scan for, say, all travel expense records with the traveler PGR, the program will find the first record that has that designation in the Traveler field. You can view the rest of the records one after another, forward and backward (by pressing **F** and **B**; see Scanning Options, below). The records will appear alphabetically in the order determined by the criteria you selected. If you enter a blank scan criteria and press **<ENTER>** or **ESC**, the program will display the first record in the database, according to the criteria you selected.

Scanning Procedures

The following process is identical for each scan option.

1. Select the criteria field on which you want to scan for records. The Scanning Criteria Input screen will then be displayed. Enter the appropriate information. Be as specific as possible, or else you may not locate the record(s) you are seeking. This is where your efforts at consistent data entry will pay off.

2. If any travel expense records match the word(s) or contraction(s) you entered, the record you are seeking will be displayed in Scanning Screen format. You can then use the options described below to edit, view, or delete the information. If there is more than one record for the name or word you input, the program will display the first one entered. You can use contractions of the name or word you are seeking and the program will find the first record matching the contractions. For example, if you only enter C for scan by name, the program will display the first record starting with the letter C.

3. If no travel expense records in the database match the name or word entered in the scan input screen, the program will display the following message:

   ```
   No records meet your criteria
   Press any key to continue
   ```

Scanning Options

Once you have located the desired travel expense record(s), you can use any of the functions listed at the bottom of the Scanning screen.

F = Forward, B = Backward. Each time you press **F**, you will browse forward from one expense record to another. To move backward through the file, press **B**. The program will move backward one record each time the **B** key is pressed. If you try to scan past the end of the file (the record most recently input), or the beginning of the file (the first record entered), the program will beep and remain on the first or last record.

E=Edit. Once you have located an expense record for editing through the Scan option, select item **E** and the system will enter full screen edit mode. Each field will be highlighted on the screen. You can move from highlighted field to highlighted field by using the cursor or by pressing **<ENTER>**. Each time you press **<ENTER>**, the cursor will advance one field. Make your changes in a field using the Backspace, Insert, and Delete keys. The editing process is ended by pressing **CTRL-END** in any field, or by pressing **<ENTER>** in the last field of the Scanning screen. Either action will save the information to disk. You can exit without saving the changes to disk by pressing the **ESC** key.

D = Delete. Deletion with the Travel Expense Reporting Program is a two-step process. First, press **D** to mark the record for deletion. MARKED FOR DELETION will appear at the bottom of the screen. Although a record is marked for deletion, it is not actually erased from the database until you use the Pack function, which is accessed from the Utilities Menu (see below). Records may remain in the marked state indefinitely. Even when you exit the program and return at a later date, records slated for deletion will still be marked.

U=Undelete. If you decide that you don't want to delete a record and you haven't used the Pack function yet, you can unmark the record for deletion by selecting the **U** option. The MARKED FOR DELETION message will then be removed from your screen.

0 = Exit. When you select the **0** option, the program will return to the Main Menu.

Generating Reports

The Travel Expense Management Program uses several report formats and organizational schemes to print your expense data. All the reports will line up properly on 8.5 x 11-inch paper using condensed (15 characters per inch) type. To create any of the reports, select Option #3, Generate Reports, from the Main Menu. The Print Menu will then be displayed, offering you two options:

1. Print entire database.
2. Print selected records.

Print Entire Database

The following steps are taken to print all the records you have entered:

1. When you choose Print Entire Database from the Print Menu, the Sort Order Selection Menu will be displayed. Choose the option by which you want the report sorted (traveler, client, department, or budget). Once the sort order is selected, the Report Selection Menu will be displayed (see below for options).

2. Select the kind of report you want from the Report Selection Menu. The reports are identical except for the subtotaling feature. Be sure to select the appropriate sort order for the desired subtotals (e.g., use the traveler sort order for the traveler report, etc.). Otherwise, you might generate confusing reports. In some cases, however, crossing reports with various sort orders can produce valuable information. The following report options are available:

   Traveler report. Contains all fields from the Travel Report Input screen, subtotaled by traveler.

   Client report. Contains all fields from the Travel Report Input screen, subtotaled by client.

   Budget report. Contains all fields from the Travel Report Input screen, subtotaled by budget code.

   Budget within department report. Contains all fields from the Travel Report Input screen, subtotaled by budget code within department code.

3. Once you have selected the type of report you want to print, a Message screen will prompt you about the report format:

   ```
   Do you want a summary report only (Y/N):
   ```

   If you select **Y**, the report will only contain subtotal information. If you select **N**, all line items will be printed.

4. Once you select the report format, the program will display the following message:

   ```
   Align printer and press enter to continue
   ```

   Make sure your printer is on-line before pressing **<ENTER>**. Otherwise you will get an error message. Retry with your printer on-line.

Print Selected Records

This option from the Print Menu allows you to select specific kinds of records to be printed. Take the following steps:

1. When you press **2**, a Report Criteria Input screen will be displayed. Notice that the screen is identical to the input screen you used to input and edit records, except that only certain fields are highlighted, and that some are expanded into ranges (see below). You can select

the records you want to filter from the database by indicating your criteria in the high-lighted fields. Any field left blank will not be included in the filter.

For example, entering A-101 in the Client field will print all records with that designation. If you wanted to further refine the list you might specify PGR in the Traveler field. This will only output records for client A-101 in which PGR was the traveler.

One caveat: To be included in the filter, a record must match all criteria you entered. So if you make the selection filter too fine by adding too many criteria, you will probably not print any records at all. Unfortunately, there is no absolute number of criteria above which the filter function defeats itself; each database has its own limits. With a little experimenta-tion, however, you will quickly determine the maximum productive levels of criteria that can be used for your data.

Note that the date field has been split into ranges. This allows you to pinpoint specific groups of travel expense records. For example, you could look for all travel records be-tween 01/01/87 and 03/31/87. If you want to select a specific date instead of a range, enter the same date in both the upper and lower limits. If you enter only half a range, only that half will be included in the criteria test. For instance, if you enter 0l/05/87 in the lower range but nothing in the upper range, all dates including 01/05/87 and beyond are con-sidered a match.

Once you have entered the criteria by which you wish to filter the database, press **CTRL-END** or **<ENTER>** in the last highlighted field. The program will then begin sear-ching for records that match your criteria.

2. If any records match your criteria, the program will display a Criteria Search Results screen, which indicates how many records met your criteria. The Criteria Search Results screen gives you the following options, in addition to pressing **ESC** to return to the Main Menu:

    Press **P** *to print*. Use this option if you wish to print out the selected records. You will be presented with the Report Selection Menu. The menu will indicate how many records are to be printed, along with the criteria you used to select them. The report formats are the same as those used to print the entire database (see above for a description). Note that when reports are printed out after a criteria search, the criteria used will be indicated at the top of the page.

    Press **S** *to display on screen*. Before you print a report, you may want to view the record to make sure you have retrieved the correct one. Or, you may just wish to review the selected records on the screen. This option allows you to do either. When you press **S**, the screen will display the first travel expense record that met your search criteria, in Scan-ning Screen format. If more than one travel expense record is found, you can page for-ward and backward through the group by using the **F** (forward) and **B** (backward). The principle is the same as that used in the editing process described above.

When you are finished examining the selected records, press **0** to return to the Report Selection Menu. You can then print the selected records, or return to the Main Menu by pressing **0**.

3. If no records are located, the program displays the message:

    ```
    No records meet your criteria
    Press any key to continue
    ```

Using Utilities

The Travel Expense Reporting Program includes four housekeeping functions. These are accessed from the Utilities Menu, which you used earlier to set up the program. The Utilities Menu is accessed by selecting Option #4 from the Main Menu. The options are described below.

Reindex. Occasionally, you may find that the search routines are not operating correctly. The most probable cause for this is a damaged index. This usually results from illegally exiting the program (see below for the proper exit routine). If this should occur, you must reindex the files by selecting Option #1 from the Utilities Menu. The reindexing option will take a variable period of time, depending on the number of records in the file and the type of computer you are using.

Pack. Packing is the final stage used to delete marked records (refer to Editing/Viewing/Deleting Records, above). Unlike marking a record, though, packing is an irreversible action; once a travel expense record is packed, it no longer exists. After selecting the pack option, the program will display how many records will be packed, and you will be asked to confirm your choice with a **Y** plus <ENTER>. The packing process can take several minutes or longer, since it must update all indexes.

Delete selected records. While the edit functions discussed earlier allows you to delete records one by one using the marking/packing functions, this option allows you to quickly delete groups of records. When you select Option #3 from the Utilities Menu, a submenu will be displayed, offering you four deletion choices: by date, traveler, department, and budget.

Option #1 deletes expense records by a range of dates. When you select this option, an input screen will be displayed, prompting you to input the date range. The remaining deletion options also call up an input screen, through which you can delete all records associated with a specific traveler, department, or budget. In each case, you will be shown the number of expense records that will be erased from the database, and asked to confirm your choice. If the number of records seems excessive, answer **N** at the confirmation, and check to make sure that records have been correctly input.

With each of the deletion options, if no records in the database meet your criteria, the program will prompt you to press a key to continue. You will then return to the Main Menu.

CAUTION: Regardless of which deletion option you choose, be certain that you wish to proceed, since the program both deletes and packs the database—once the records are removed from the database, there is no way to retrieve them! Before using any of the delete functions, you would be well advised to back up your .dbf files, just in case you change your mind or discover that certain records are still needed. In any case, make sure you have a recent printout of the entire database.

System setup. The Travel Expense Reporting Program uses the dBXL To Go basic setup options. These are described in Chapter 1.

Note: If you want to delete all records and start with a clean database, you can either recopy the .dbf files from your distribution diskette or use the dBXL Zap command to erase all records. Zap simultaneously deletes and packs all records in your database. To use Zap, make current the directory in which you keep your Travel Expense Reporting Program files. Start dBXL, and at the command prompt type:

```
use travel
```

Next, type:

```
zap
```

dBXL will ask you to confirm the action with a **Y** or **N**. When you select **Y**, all records will be erased and deleted from your database. After zapping, you must reindex to ensure that your indexes correspond to the program.

CAUTION: Zap is an irrevocable command; there is no way to recover a zapped file. Therefore, back up your data before zapping it!

Exiting

It is vitally important that you properly exit from the Travel Expense Reporting Program. Failure to do so may cause file or index damage. While it is often possible to remedy the situation by reindexing, the damage may be permanent, in which case you must start over again by copying the files from your working diskette and re-entering your data, or restoring your database from your most recent backup copy. Given the needless waste of time and the aggravation in reconstructing a database, *always exit by pressing* **0** *in the menu you are working with until you reach the Main Menu.* Pressing **0** at the Main Menu will close all database files and return you to a Sign-Off screen that asks you if you wish to leave the program. Entering **Y** returns you to DOS. Entering **N** returns you to the Main Menu. Note: If you are running an uncompiled program, pressing **X** will return you to the dBXL prompt.

9 Manual For Sales Lead Management Program

Features

- Menu driven.
- Password protection.
- Complete system for tracking sales leads from initial inquiry to sale.
- Allows for analysis of marketing/advertising sources.
- Keeps track of company representatives assigned to each sales lead.
- Comprehensive reporting system.
- Sorts sales leads by inquiry type, model, source type, source code, region, customer, and representative.
- Prints sales representative follow-up reports, including suggested action.

Contents

Introduction

This program enables you to track and manage sales leads for your company's various product lines. In addition, it generates management reports for analytical purposes, as well as current prospect lists for your sales force. The input screen allows you to enter detailed demographic information as well as information about the source of the lead and the follow-up action from your sales or customer service representatives. The program makes it easy to maintain an active database by allowing you to evaluate the sales potential of each lead, and to purge leads that are unlikely to result in further action.

Sales lead data can be output in a number of formats, either for the entire database or for user-selected criteria. The reports include:

1. Summary report. Gives you all the data in compact form.
2. Detailed report. Prints out all information as it was entered into the database.
3. Source report. Breaks down leads by source type and source code.
4. Sales rep report. Prints a list of leads assigned to each sales representative.

All functions of the program are accessed by menus that include instructions on the bottom of the screen. These menus allow you to customize the sales lead report header and printer specifications, establish passwords, scan records, print reports, and update the sales lead file using various file utilities and edit functions.

Before using the program, read through this manual and familiarize yourself with all the input, report, and utility functions. You may want to set up a practice sales lead system, using two or three lead records to review the functions of the program. Also, create a backup disk for your database file (lead.dbf). there's no need to back up your program (.prg), format (.fmt), or report (.frm) files. You can always recopy them from your working diskette. You don't have to back up your index files either, since your program creates them if they aren't found in the directory.

At a minimum, back up your .dbf files each time you add or edit records; the few minutes the procedure requires will more than offset the time you would need to spend if the entire database had to be recreated. Remember, no hardware system is infallible, and it's better to be safe than sorry!

Finally, if you are an experienced dBXL user and wish to modify the program, refer to the Technical Specifications section charts and tables. You will find a menu tree diagram, a program tree that lists the calling program hierarchy, and a table that describes the characteristics of each field.

Data Entry Keys

After you have input data, you may use the Backspace key to erase your entry (provided that you haven't pressed <ENTER>). Alternately, you can use the cursor and Delete/Insert keys to modify your entry. When you do press <ENTER>, the cursor will move to the next data input field. If you need to return to a previous entry, use the up cursor key to move the cursor to the desired field. Enter your changes and press <ENTER> to move on through the input screen. Note that any errors made during data entry can also be corrected later by means of the Edit option (discussed below).

Installing and Setting up the Program

Before you begin using the Sales Lead Management Program, you will have to install and set it up. General instructions for installation and setup are contained in Chapter 1.

Starting the Program

The easiest way to start the Sales Lead Management Program is to create a batch file. You can also start the program manually by typing:

```
do lead
```

after starting dBXL (see Chapter 1 for specifics of both startup techniques).

Regardless of how you begin the Sales Lead Management Program, you will first see the dBXL copyright and license notice. The screen will display the message "Creating indexes, please wait". This process may require a few seconds, but only occurs the first time you run the program after installation. The Sales Lead Program Main Menu will then appear.

Creating a Sales Lead Record

All information is entered through the Sales Lead Input screen, which is called up by select-ing Option #1, Add Records, from the Main Menu. The Sales Lead Input screen consists of three sections:

Customer demographics section. Provides fields for basic information about the customer submitting the lead.

Lead/source data section. Contains information about the product the customer is interested in, and the type of response he would like from your company (phone call, information, or demo). In addition, this section allows you to describe the source of the lead so you can later analyze the effectiveness of your marketing and PR campaigns.

Action section. Indicates which sales rep will follow up on the lead, the quality of the lead, the date for which followup is scheduled, and whether or not a sale was made.

Customer Demographics Section

When you select Add Records from the Main Menu, the cursor will move through the following sequence of fields each time you press **<ENTER>**.

1. Name: You may enter records as last name first or first name first. You will probably find it easier to scan (see below) for records if they are last name first. In any case, be consistent; Smith, John L. (period after the L) is treated differently than Smith, John L (no period after the L).
2. Title:
3. Company:
4. Address:
5. City: (fields for state and zip follow on the same line, but are not labeled)
6. Telephone:

Lead/Source Data Section

This part of the screen is divided into three subsections.

INQUIRY

Type. This field can be used one of two ways: to describe the lead (e.g., walk-in, telephone, written response), or the type of equipment (e.g., computer equipment, telephone system, photocopier, etc).

Model. If relevant, enter the model number of the product related to the inquiry.

Desc. If desired, give a brief description of the product or product line in question.

Date. Enter the date the sales lead was received.

Amount. If known, enter the approximate amount the customer intends to spend.

SOURCE

The following fields are related to the source that generated the sales lead. The first two fields, Type and Code, are extremely useful in assessing the effectiveness of various marketing sources.

Type. This field is used to designate the general source category, such as a space advertisement, a direct mail piece, a radio or television spot, a trade show, and so on. It is very important to be consistent in the way you input data in this field, or else your reports will not accurately group similar source types together. For example, sales lead records with the source type SPACE AD will not appear together on reports with records that have source type entered as SPACE AD. (with a period) or SPACE ADS (plural). Periods, commas, and spaces are all treated as characters.

Given the precision that is called for, you are probably best off creating codes rather than using abbreviated or truncated words. If you use 01 to indicate space ads, the chance of inconsistencies are minimized. Coding schemes also have the advantage of providing for easy extension. For example, 01N could refer to newspaper ads, 01M could refer to magazine ads, and so on.

Whether you use abbreviations or codes, we recommend that you keep a list of "official" spellings and codes near the computer. This will ensure that everyone who inputs sales leads records plays by the same rules.

Code. The code field allows you to make the Type field more specific. For example, SA-PCTIME might stand for a space ad in *PC Time Magazine* (the date the ad was run can be entered in the Date field; see below). The advantage of having separate Type and Code fields is that you can break out whole classes of source types in the reports (print ads, direct mail, etc.), as well as individual source items (the space ad in *PC Time Magazine*, the February 1987 direct mail campaign, etc.; see reports section, below).

Again, it is critically important that you input codes consistently; SA-PCTIME will not be grouped together on reports with SA-PC TIME (a space before TIME). As in the case of the Type field, you would be wise to keep a list of all current codes by the computer.

Desc. You can use this field to describe the source. For example, if the code in the previous field refers to an ad in *PC Time Magazine*, you might enter Full Pg, 4 Color, or some other description. If the code refers to a direct mail campaign, you might enter something like 200KM, $65/$95, to describe a 200,000-piece mailing, with offers of $65 and $95. If you do plan on using the field, choose the shortest explanation that gives the most information.

Date. This field is used to designate when an ad was run, when direct mail pieces were dropped at the post office, when a trade show began, and so on.

Cost. Enter the cost of the ad space, the mailing, or whatever medium you used. Totals for this field are shown in the various reports (see below).

REQUEST

The three fields in this subsection are used to indicate what the customer is requesting from your company.

Contact. If the customer wants a phone call from a sales rep, enter Y. The date field following the contact can be used to either indicate when the customer would like the call, or when the call was made. You can decide which is more appropriate for your type of business.

Info Only. If the customer only wants literature, enter Y. The adjacent date field can then be used to indicate when the material was sent.

Demo. Use this field to indicate whether the customer requested a demonstration. The date field can either be used to indicate the scheduled date, or the date the demo took place.

Action Section

This part of the input screen is used to track the routing of the lead and whether or not it eventually led to a sale. It is divided into three subsections.

ASSIGNMENT

Region. If appropriate, enter the customer's sales region.

Territory. Subset of region.

Representative. Enter the sales rep's initials or number.

Date. Use this field to indicate when the lead was assigned to the appropriate sales rep.

STATUS

Rating. This field allows you to rate the likelihood of a lead resulting in a sale. The sales reps can use this information when determining the priority of follow-up calls. The field will accommodate up to two digits, so you can use 1 to 10 or 20, or whatever ranges are appropriate.

Followup. This is an all-purpose field that you can use to either indicate when a followup is scheduled or when one took place.

RESULT

Sale. Use this field to enter whether a sale was made or not (**Y** or **N**).

Amount. If a sale was made, enter the amount.

Active. This field is used in cleaning out the database. The default response is **Y**. When the lead is no longer of value, or has not resulted in any further action, you may want to change its status to inactive by typing **N**. You can then use the Delete function (see Utilities) to purge it from the file.

Adding Another Sales Lead Record

When you press **<ENTER>** while the cursor is in the Active field, or press **CTRL-END** elsewhere during data input, the record will be included in the database. A prompt at the bottom of the screen will then ask if you want to add another record. To accept the default **Y** and continue adding records, press **<ENTER>**. If you enter **N**, the program will return to the Main Menu. Note: Each sales lead record must have, at a minimum, an item or a client to be included in the database.

Editing/Viewing/Deleting Records

The Scan Function

To recall a previously created sales lead record, select Edit/Delete Records from the Main Menu (Option #2), and choose a criteria by which you will scan for records in the database.

Scanning is used to search for a record or group of records, and then to display them on the screen. It is useful for two purposes. First, it will enable you to pinpoint a specific record for viewing, editing, or deleting, as explained below. Second, you can locate a group of records, after which you can display them one by one for editing or deletion.

One way to think of the second scan function is to imagine the records on a track. When you scan for, say, all sales lead records with the source type 01, the program will find the first record that has that designation in the Type field. You can view the rest of the records one after another, forward and backward (by pressing **F** and **B**; see editing options, below). The records will appear alphabetically in the order determined by the criteria you selected. If you enter a blank scan criteria and press **<ENTER>** or **ESC**, the program will display the first record in the database, according to the criteria you selected.

Scanning Procedures

The following process is identical for each scan option.

1. Select the criteria field on which you want to scan for records. The Scanning Criteria Input screen will then be displayed. Enter the appropriate information. You can use contractions of the name you are seeking and the program will find the first record matching the contractions. For example, if you only enter C for a scan by name, the program will display the first record starting with the letter C.

2. If any sales lead records match the word(s) or contraction(s) you entered, the record you are seeking will be displayed in Scanning Screen format (see below). You can then use the options described below to edit, view, or delete the information. If there is more than one record for the name or word you input, the program will display the first one entered. If you entered a contraction of a name or word, the program will display records in the order determined by the entire field. For example, if you scan on Wes in the Customer field, records with Westfield and Westlake will be found. Westfield will appear first though, because it precedes Westlake alphabetically.

3. If no sales lead records in the database match the name or word entered in the scan input screen, the program will display the following message:

    ```
    No records meet your criteria
    Press any key to continue
    ```

Scanning Options

Once you have located the desired sales lead record(s), you can use any of the functions listed at the bottom of the Scanning screen.

F = Forward, B = Backward. Each time you press **F**, you will browse forward from one sales lead record to another. To move backward through the file, press **B**. The program will move backward one record each time the **B** key is pressed. If you try to scan past the end of the file (the record most recently input), or the beginning of the file (the first record entered), the program will beep and remain on the last or first record.

E=Edit. Once you have located a sales lead record for editing through the Scan option, select item **E** and the system will enter full screen edit mode. Each field will be highlighted on the screen. You can move from highlighted field to highlighted field by using the cursor or by pressing **<ENTER>**. Each time you press **<ENTER>**, the cursor will advance one field. Make your changes in a field using the Backspace, Insert, and Delete keys. The editing process is ended by pressing **CTRL-END** in any field, or by pressing **<ENTER>** in the last field of the Edit screen. Either action will save the information to disk. You can exit without saving the changes to disk by pressing the **ESC** key.

D=Delete. Deletion with the Sales Lead Management Program is a two-step process. First, press **D** to mark the record for deletion. MARKED FOR DELETION will appear at the bottom of the screen. Although a record is marked for deletion, it is not actually erased from the database until you use the Pack function, which is accessed from the Utilities Menu (see below). Records may remain in the marked state indefinitely. Even when you exit the program and return at a later date, records slated for deletion will still be marked.

U = Undelete. If you decide that you don't want to delete a record and you haven't used the Pack function yet, you can unmark the record for deletion by selecting the **U** option. The MARKED FOR DELETION message will then be removed from your screen.

0 = Exit. When you select the **0** option, the program will return to the Main Menu.

Generating Reports

The Sales Lead Management Program uses several report formats and organizational schemes to print your sales lead data. All of the reports will line up properly on 8.5 x 1 l-inch paper using condensed (15 characters per inch) type. To create any of the reports, select Generate Reports (Option #3) from the Main Menu. The Print Menu will then be displayed, offering you two options:

1. Print entire database.

2. Print selected records.

Print Entire Database

Take the following steps to print all the records you have entered:

1. When you choose Print Entire Database from the Print Menu, a Sort Order Selection Menu will be displayed. Choose the option by which you want the report sorted. Once the sort order is selected, the Report Selection Menu will be displayed (see below for options). Be sure to select a sort option that is logical for the report you wish to generate. For example, you should probably select the Source sort order for the Source Report, and the Rep sort order for the Rep Report; otherwise, you may generate confusing reports. In some cases, however, crossing report types with various sort orders can produce valuable special printouts. Experiment for yourself and determine which combinations yield the most useful reports.

2. Select the kind of report you want from the Report Selection Menu, which offers the following options:

   Summary report. Contains all fields, organized in compact form. The Summary Report prints eight sales leads per page. (Suggested sort order: any.)

   Detailed report. Presents the same information as the Summary Report, but it is displayed exactly as it appears on the screen, two per page. Use this report when you need space between entries to annotate or edit the data. (Suggested sort order: any.)

   Source report. Breaks down leads by source type and code. Includes Source Type, Code, Desc, Date, and Cost; Inquiry Type, Model, Desc, Date, and Amount; Sale Made (Y/N), and Sale Amount. Source Cost, Inquiry Amount, and Sale Amount are totaled, so you can determine the cost effectiveness of various lead sources. (Suggested sort order: source.)

   Sales rep report. Shows Sales Rep identifier and Lead Rating, as well as the Customer Name, Company, Telephone, Inquiry Type, Date, Amount, Type of request (Contact, Info, Demo) and Follow Up. (Suggested sort order: sales rep.)

3. Once you have selected the type of report you want to print, a Message screen will prompt you to:

   ```
   Align printer and press enter to continue.
   ```

   Make sure your printer is on-line before pressing **<ENTER>**. Otherwise you will get an error message. Retry with your printer on-line.

Print Selected Records

This option from the Print Menu allows you to select specific kinds of records to be printed. Take the following steps:

1. When you press 2, a Report Criteria Input screen will be displayed. Notice that the screen is identical to the input screen you used to input and edit records, with the exception that

only certain fields are highlighted, and some are expanded into ranges (see below). You can select the records you want to filter from the database by indicating your criteria in the highlighted fields. Any field left blank will not be included in the filter.

For example, entering SPACE AD in the Source Type field will print all records with those words in that field. If you wanted to further refine the list you might specify PCM for *PC Magazine*. This will only output space ads associated with *PC Magazine*. Since the program matches records against whatever letters you input in the criteria fields, PCM will be a match for PCMJAN86, PCMFEB86, PCMJUL86, and so on.

One caveat: To be included in the filter, a record must match *all* criteria you entered. So if you make the selection filter too fine by adding too many criteria, you will probably not print any records at all. Unfortunately, there is no absolute number of criteria above which the filter function defeats itself; each database has its own limits. With a little experimentation, however, you will quickly determine the maximum productive levels of criteria that can be used for your data.

Note that the Date and Amount fields in each section of the input screen are split into ranges, as is the Lead Rating field. This allows you to pinpoint specific groups of leads—for example, all inquiries between 01/01/87 and 03/31/87, all resulting sales of $5,000 to $10,000, or all leads with a quality rating 5 to 10. If you want to select a specific value instead of a range, enter the same number in both the upper and the lower limits. Let's say you want to find all leads on January 5, 1987; you would enter 01/05/87 in both fields. The same holds true with the Rating and other fields displayed as ranges in the criteria screen. If you enter only half a range, only that half will be included in the criteria test. For instance, if you entered 5000 in the lower range but nothing in the upper range, all values including 5000 and above would be considered a match.

Once you have entered the criteria by which you wish to filter the database, press **CTRL-END** or <ENTER> in the last highlighted field. The program will then begin searching for records that match your criteria.

2. If any records do match your criteria, the program will display the Criteria Search Results screen which indicates how many records met your criteria. The Criteria Search Results screen gives you the following options, in addition to pressing **ESC** to return to the Main Menu:

    *Press **P** to print*. Use this option if you wish to print out the selected records. You will be presented with the Report Selection Menu. The menu will indicate how many records are to be printed, along with criteria you used to select them. The report formats are the same as those used to print the entire database (see above for a description). Note that when reports are printed out after a criteria search, the criteria used will be indicated at the top of the page.

    *Press **S** to display on screen*. Before you print a report, you may want to view the sales lead records to make sure you have retrieved the correct one(s). Or, you may just wish to review the selected records on the screen. This option allows you to do either. When you press **S**, the screen will display the first sales lead record that met your search criteria, in Scanning Screen format. If more than one lead is found, you can page forward and backward through the selected records by using **F** (forward) and **B** (backward). The principle is the same as that used in the editing process described above.

When you are finished examining the selected records, press **0** to return to the Report Selection Menu. You can then print the selected records, or return to the Main Menu by pressing **0**.

3. If no records are located, the program displays the message:

```
No records meet your criteria
Press any key to continue
```

Using Utilities

The Sales Lead Management Program includes four housekeeping functions. These are accessed from the Utilities Menu, which you used earlier to set up the program. The Utilities Menu is accessed by selecting Option #4 from the Main Menu. The options are described below.

Reindex. Occasionally, you may find that the search routines are not operating correctly. The most probable cause for this is a damaged index. This usually results from illegally exiting the program (see below for the proper exit routine). If this should occur, you must reindex the files by selecting Option #1 from the Utilities Menu. The reindexing option will take a variable period of time, depending on the number of records in the file and the type of computer you are using.

Pack. Packing is the final stage used to delete marked records (refer to Editing/Viewing/Deleting Records, above). Unlike marking a record, though, packing is irreversible; once a sales lead record is packed, it no longer exists. After selecting the pack option, the program will display how many records will be packed, and you will be asked to confirm your choice with a **Y** plus an **<ENTER>**. The packing process can take several minutes or longer, since it must update all indexes.

Delete selected records. While the edit functions discussed earlier allow you to delete records one by one using the marking/packing functions, this option allows you to quickly delete groups of records. When you select Option #3 from the Utilities Menu, a submenu will be displayed, offering you three deletion choices: inactive records, info-only records, and sales leads with ratings below a user-specified number.

Inactive sales leads are those in which you entered an **N** in the Active field on the input screen. Info-only leads have a **Y** in the Info-Only field. You might want to delete them periodically to reduce the size of your database. When you select Delete Inactive Records or Delete Info-Only Records, the program will indicate how many leads are slated for deletion.

Confirm the function with a **Y**, or press **N** to return to the Utilities Menu (if the number of leads to be deleted seems excessive, terminate the deletion process and check to make sure that they were correctly input).

Option #3 deletes leads of a specified rating. When you select this option, an input screen will be displayed, prompting you to input a rating. All records with ratings below that entered will be removed from the database if you choose to complete the delete function. As with the other deletion options, you will be shown the number of leads that will be erased from the database, and asked to confirm your choice.

With each of the above options, the program will indicate that no records were deleted, and prompt you to press a key to continue if no records in the database meet your deletion criteria. You will then return to the Delete Selected Records Menu (or Main Menu).

> **CAUTION:** Regardless of which deletion option you choose, be certain that you wish to proceed; once the records are deleted, there is no way to retrieve them! Before using any of the delete functions, you would be well advised to back up your .dbf files, just in case you change your mind or discover that certain records are still needed. In any case, make sure you have a recent printout of the entire database.

System setup. The Sales Lead Program uses the dBXL To Go basic setup options. These are described in Chapter 1.

Note: If you want to delete all records and start with a clean database, you can either recopy the .dbf files from your distribution diskette or use the dBXL Zap command to erase all records. Zap simultaneously deletes and packs all records in your database. To use Zap, make current the directory in which you keep your Sales Lead Management Program files. Start dBXL, and at the command prompt type:

```
use lead
```

Next, type:

```
zap
```

dBXL will ask you to confirm the action with a **Y** or **N**. When you select **Y**, all records will be erased and deleted from your database. After zapping, you must reindex to ensure that your indexes correspond to the program.

> **CAUTION**: Zap is an irrevocable command, and there is no way to recover a zapped file. Therefore, back up your data before zapping it!

Exiting

It is vitally important that you properly exit from the Sales Lead Management Program. Failure to do so may cause file or index damage. While it is often possible to remedy the situation by reindexing, the damage may be permanent, in which case you must start over again by copying the files from your working diskette and re-entering your data, or restoring your database from your most recent backup copy. Given the needless waste of time and the aggravation in reconstructing a database, *always exit by pressing* **0** *in the menu you are working with until you reach the Main Menu.* Pressing **0** at the Main Menu will close all database files and return you to a Sign-Off screen that asks you if you wish to leave the program. Entering **Y** returns you to DOS. Entering **N** returns you to the Main Menu. Note: If you are running an uncompiled program, pressing **X** will return you to the dBXL prompt.

10 Manual For Bibliography Program

Features

- Menu driven.
- Password protection.
- Detailed input screen allows input of all information needed to generate professional bibliographies of books and magazine in *The Chicago Manual of Style* format.
- Allows user to organize bibliographies by author, title, subject, topic, footnote number, or a customized numerical ordering system.
- Key word search.
- Unlimited size abstracts.
- Eight types of summary and detail reports. Bibliography automatically distinguishes between periodical and book formats.
- Enter bibliographic citations as abstracts in a simple word processing mode.

Contents

Introduction

This program enables you to easily prepare a comprehensive bibliography or footnote list that includes subjects, topics, article or book titles, publication or publishers' names, and the date and volume number of each reference. In addition to entering brief notes in the comment field at the bottom of each record, you can create an abstract of any length.

You'll not only find the Bibliography Program helpful in preparing your reference list, but in organizing your research. Even if you aren't writing a book, article, or paper, the program can be extremely valuable in tracking certain trends you read about in the literature of your field, because you can generate selective citation lists based on key words in each article. These lists can then assist you in your market research, product development, or business planning efforts.

Other uses for the program include cataloging product or book reviews and organizing the holdings of a small personal or business library. The key words search ability makes it possible to create a sophisticated cross-referencing system for topics or publications. In addition, the program gives you the ability to create your own numbering system, so you can assign appropriate identifiers to each record.

The Bibliography Program offers eight basic reports:

1. Summary report. Prints compact versions of all citations.

2. Detailed report. Prints out all information (except the abstract) as it was entered into the database.

3. Abstract report. Prints abstracts.

4. Bibliography report. Outputs a bibliography according to formats listed in *The Chicago Manual of Style*.

5. Footnote report. Organizes citations by footnote number.

6. Topic report. Organizes the citations by topic headings.

7. Subject report. Prints out citations by subject headings.

8. Subject within topic report. Outputs citations by topic headings, then by subject headings. All functions of the program are accessed by menus that include instructions on the bottom of the screen. These menus allow you to customize the bibliography report header and printer specifications, establish passwords, scan and edit records, print reports, and maintain the database using various utility functions.

Before using the program, read through this manual and familiarize yourself with all the input, report, and utility functions. You may want to set up a practice bibliography, using two or three citation records to review the functions of the program. Also, create a backup disk for your database and abstract files (Bibl.dbf and Bibl.dbt). There's no need to back up your program (.prg), format (.fmt), or report (.frm) files. You can always recopy them from your working diskette. You don't have to back up your index files either, since your program creates them if they aren't found in the directory.

At a minimum, back up your .dbf and .dbt files each time you add or edit records; the few minutes the procedure requires will more than offset the time you would need to spend if the entire database had to be recreated. Remember, no hardware system is infallible, and it's better to be safe than sorry!

Finally, if you are an experienced dBXL user and wish to modify the program, refer to the Technical Specifications tables and charts. You will find a menu tree diagram, a program tree that lists the calling program hierarchy, and a table that describes the characteristics of each field.

Data Entry Keys

After you have input data, you may use the Backspace key to erase your entry (provided that you haven't pressed <ENTER>). Alternately, you can use the cursor and Delete/Insert keys to modify your entry. When you do press <ENTER>, the cursor will move to the next data input field. If you need to return to a previous entry, use the up cursor key to move the cursor to the desired field. Enter your changes and press <ENTER> to move on through the input screen. Note that any errors made during data entry can also be corrected later by means of the Edit option (see below).

Installing and Setting up the Program

Before you begin using the Bibliography Program, you will have to install and set it up. General instructions for installation and setup are contained in Chapter 1.

Starting the Program

The easiest way to start the Bibliography Program is to create a batch file. You can also start the program manually by typing:

```
do biblio
```

after starting dBXL (see Chapter 1 for specifics of both startup techniques).

Regardless of how you begin the Bibliography Program, you will first see the dBXL copyright and license notice. The screen will display the message "Creating indexes, please wait." This process may require a few seconds, but it only occurs the first time you run the program after installation. The Bibliography Program Main Menu will then appear.

Creating a Bibliography

All data is entered into the program through the Bibliography Input screen, which is called up by selecting Option #1, Add Records, from the Main Menu. The input screen consists of three sections.

1. Topic/Subject description section. Contains information about the subject matter and citation order.

2. Citation section. Detailed information about the citation.

3. Comment section. Brief free-form comment about the citation.

   In the following descriptions of each section, the characteristics of each field are described. The fields are listed in the order in which the cursor will proceed each time you press **<ENTER>**. When you reach the last field in the input screen, Abstract (memo), and press **<ENTER>**, the record will be saved to the database. Alternately, you can save a record at any point in the input screen by pressing **CTRL-END**. You can exit from the input screen by pressing **ESC**.

Topic/Subject Section

Abstract (memo). The Bibliography Program allows you to enter an abstract for a book or article either before or after you enter the detailed bibliographic information. On the input screen, you will notice that the Abstract (memo) field appears in two places: in the top left-hand corner and the bottom left-hand corner of your screen.

To enter an abstract, press **CTRL-PgDn** when the cursor is in the highlighted field occupied by the word *memo*. The dBXL Text Editor Help screen will replace the bibliography input form, and the cursor will be under the left-hand corner of the Help Screen border. The text editor functions are listed in the Help screen.

(Note: if you are a WordStar user, you will be right at home with the dBXL text editing commands). Consult your dBXL manual for additional details.

The abstract can be as long as you like. When you are finished, press **CTRL-END** or **CTRL-W**. This will save the abstract into the database and redisplay the Bibliography Input screen. If you wish to exit the abstract without saving it, press **ESC**. dBXL will then prompt you as to whether you wish to abort editing. Respond with **Y**.

Type. Enter a designation for whether the source is a book or a journal. You can also make up your own coding scheme. You might want to add newspapers or dissertations, for example. Whatever system you devise, though, bear in mind that the bibliography format is designed for either books or journal articles, in the format prescribed in *The Chicago Manual of Style*. The Type field is especially useful, since you can later use the coding scheme as a criterion for printing out lists of specific kinds of citations, such as all books, all journals, dissertations, kinds of records, and so on. Note: The bibliography report uses a book format for all entries of Type = B, and a periodical format for all others.

Order. The Order field allows you to specify where a particular citation will be located in the bibliography. While the program also gives you the option of organizing a bibliography by author, title, topic, subject, or footnote, the Order field allows you to be more specific. For example, your ordering system might simply start with 1 and progress up one digit for each citation. Later, you might decide that three citations belong between number 9 and number 10. Use the decimal point to create 9.1, 9.2, and 9.3. In this way, you can control the order in which citations are output. This can be particularly useful when organizing the citations into a logical order for your paper or project.

Footnote. This field allows you to assign a footnote number to the citation. Later, using the report generator, you can create a list of citations ordered by footnote number. You should not enter footnote numbers until you are certain of the final sequence. Otherwise, you will have to edit each record.

Topic. Enter the broadest general category that covers the bibliography. For purposes of illustration, we'll use Health Care Cost Reduction. Note: Be absolutely consistent with each entry, or else you will not be able to accurately subgroup records later on. If you input Health Care Cost Reduction on some of the records, Health Care Costs, on others, and Cost Reduction on still others, you will get three separate topics although you only wanted one when you go to produce a report organized by topic. One way to avoid mistakes is to keep a topic list by the computer. The topic list should note all punctuation and abbreviations as well as correct spellings.

Subject. Enter the specific subject of the article or book for example: HMO's (Health Maintenance Organizations). Again, to-the-letter consistency is critical: HMOs (no apostrophe) will be treated differently than HMO's (with apostrophe); they will not be grouped together on your reports. Further, if you entered HMO on some records and H.M.O. (with periods) on others, you will not be able to locate all desired records when you use the Scan function (see Editing/Viewing/Deleting Citations and Abstracts, below). Keeping a subject list by the computer will help ensure that your entries are consistent.

Key words. You may enter up to four key words that identify the content of the article or book. Separate each key word with a space or comma. You can later use the report generator to select those citations that have one or more of the words input in the Key Word field. Let's continue our health care cost example. You have been entering articles that discuss Diagnosis Related Groups (DRGs) and specifically mention appendectomies, and you wish to later create a list of all articles that include those two terms. You could enter DRGs and appendectomies as key words, and later specify that you would like a report that will *only* include records with *both* those words in the Key words field. The more sophisticated your key word scheme, the more you can specifically filter records from the database. Consistency, of course, will be important: DRG and D.R.G. (with periods) will be considered different words.

Citation Section

Author(s). Enter the author(s) or editor(s) name(s), paying attention to consistency. Remember, Smith, AL will be treated differently than Smith, A.L. (with periods). Similarly, Smith AL, Weston BJ and Frank G (no comma after Weston) will not be treated the same as Smith AL, Weston BJ, and Frank G (comma after Weston). Specifically, when the records containing these authors are printed, they may not be grouped together. Before entering any records, establish how you intend to input author's names, and stick to it! Note: The Author field prints exactly as entered; the style used for this field will be used to print your bibliography.

Title. This field allows you to enter up to two lines for the title and subtitle. Note that the cursor will not wrap like a word processor. That means you must press **<ENTER>** to move the cursor to the next line. If you begin typing a word and find that it breaks in an incorrect place for a hyphen, use the Backspace or cursor and Delete keys to modify your entry. Then press **<ENTER>** and continue onto the next line.

Publication. Consistency is again an important issue, not only from a standpoint of form and aesthetics, but in terms of your ability to group together all records from the same publisher. *Am.J. of Health Care* (with periods) will not be grouped together with *Am J of Health Care* (no periods) or with *Am J Health Care* (no "of").

Volume. Enter the volume number if you are dealing with a periodical. Note: Do not use this field if you are inputting a book citation; it will not appear in the bibliography report. If you wish to indicate the volume for a book citation, include it in the title.

Number. Enter the periodical number.

Issue. This field can include a maximum of a three-character month, and the full date (e.g., May 1967).

Pages. You may use any style or conventions you wish to note pages, a range of pages, or a mixture of both, such as: 12,13,15; 321-345; or 23, 54, 87-98.

Publisher. As in all fields that can be used as a criterion for creating lists, be consistent when you enter data. HB Books, Inc., will not be grouped together with HB Books Inc (no comma after Books or period after Inc.) or with HB Books (no Inc).

City. Enter the book publisher's location.

Date. Enter the publication date of the book.

Comment Section

Comment. This field allows you to make a notation, such as "Good source of current figures," "Excellent graphs," "Opposing view," "Available in law library," and so on. You may also leave it blank if you wish. Note that the data in the Comment field cannot be searched or sorted, so it is not interchangeable with the Key words field.

Abstract (memo). This field is identical to the Abstract (memo) field described above. Press **CTRL-PgDn** to create an abstract, **CTRL-END** or **CTRL-W** to save an abstract, or **ESC** to abandon an abstract without saving it. The reason Abstract (memo) appears twice on the screen, as the first and last fields, is that logically you will want to enter an abstract after you have input the citation information. When you later edit or view a record on screen, however, you do not want to have to press **<ENTER>** 20 times before you can press **CTRL-PgDn** and display the abstract. Hence the dual position of the field.

Adding Another Record

When you press **<ENTER>** while the cursor is in the Abstract (memo) field, or press **CTRL-END** elsewhere during data input, the record will be included in the database. A prompt at the bottom of the screen will then ask if you want to add another record. To accept the default, **Y**, and continue adding records, press **<ENTER>**. If you enter **N**, the program will return to the Main Menu.

Editing/Reviewing/Deleting Citations and Abstracts

The Scan Function

To recall a previously created bibliography record, select the Edit/Delete Records option from the Main Menu (Option # 2), and choose a criterion by which you will scan for records in the database.

Scanning is used to search for a record or group of records, and then to display them on the screen. It is useful for two purposes. First, it will enable you to pinpoint a specific record for viewing, editing, or deleting, as explained below. Second, you can locate a group of records and display them one by one for editing or deletion.

One way to think of the second scan function is to imagine the records organized along a track. When you scan for, say, all articles with Heath Care Cost Reduction as a subject, the program will find the first record that has those words in that exact order in the subject field. You can view the rest of the records one after another, forward and backward (by pressing **F** and **B**; see editing options, below). The records will appear alphabetically in the order determined by the criteria you selected. If you enter a blank scan criteria and press **<ENTER>** or **ESC**, the program will display the first record in the database, according to the criteria you selected.

Note: You can use contractions of the name you are seeking and the program will find the first record matching the contractions. For example, if you only enter C for a scan by name, the program will display the first record starting with the letter C.

Scanning Procedures

The following process is identical for each scan option.

1. Select the criteria field by which you want to scan for records. A Scanning Criteria Input screen will then be displayed. Enter the appropriate information. Note: When you are looking for a specific citation, be as specific as possible. That means choosing the most specific scan criteria, such as title, author, or footnote number. Be as precise as you can in terms of your data input. If you are looking for an article by Smith, V.L., simply entering Smith will locate every Smith in the database, and you will have to page through them all to find the one that you want.

   If you wish to edit, view, or delete a group of citations, use more general criteria, such as subject or topic. You could use this approach to group all records with, say, the topic Health Care Cost Reduction, or the subject HMO's. Once the records are found, you can page through them one by one, edit them, or mark them for deletion by using the editing options described below.

2. If any records match the word(s) or contraction(s) you entered, the record you are seeking will be displayed in a special Scanning Screen format. Once a record is in Scanning Screen format, you can use any of the editing, viewing, or deletion options described below. If there is more than one record for the name or word you input, the program will display the first one entered. If you entered a contraction of a name or word, the program will display records in the order determined by the entire field. For example, if you scan on Wes in the author field, records with Wesley and West will be found. The one with Wesley will appear first though, because it alphabetically precedes West.

3. If no records in the database match the name or word entered in the Scanning Criteria Input screen, the program will display the following message:

```
No records meet your criteria
Press any key to continue
```

Scanning Options

Once you have located the desired record(s), you can use any of the functions listed at the bottom of the Scanning screen:

T = Text. If you select **T**, the program will redisplay the Edit screen, this time with a highlighted memo field. You can edit or view the abstract by pressing **CTRL-PgDn**. When you have made the necessary changes, press **CTRL-END** or **CTRL-W**. If you have only viewed the abstract, or decided that you don't want to save the changes, press **ESC** *twice* and the record will reappear in the Scanning Screen format. Press **ESC** again to return to the Main Menu.

F = Forward, B = Backward. Each time you press **F**, you will browse forward from one record to another. To move backward through the file, press **B**. The program will move backward one record each time the **B** key is pressed. If you try to scan past the end of the file (the record most recently input), or the beginning of the file (the first record entered), the program will beep and remain on the last or first record.

E=Edit. Once you have located a record for editing through the Scan option, select item **E** and the program will enter full screen edit mode. Each field will be highlighted on the screen. You can move from highlighted field to highlighted field by using the cursor keys or pressing **<ENTER>**, just as you did when you initially entered the record into the Bibliography Input screen. Make your changes in a field using the Backspace, Insert, and Delete keys. The editing process is ended by pressing **CTRL-END** in any field, or by pressing **<ENTER>** in the last field. Either action will save the information to disk. You can exit without saving the changes to disk by pressing the **ESC** key. Note: You must use the **T = Text** option described above to gain access to the abstract.

D=Delete. Deletion with the Bibliography Program is a two-step process. First, press **D** to mark the record for deletion. MARKED FOR DELETION will appear above the menu options. Although a record is marked for deletion, it is not actually deleted until you use the Pack function, which is accessed from the Utilities Menu (see below). Records may remain in the marked state indefinitely. Even when you exit the program and return at a later date, records slated for deletion will still be marked.

U=Undelete. If you decide that you don't want to delete a record and you haven't used the Pack function yet, you can unmark the record for deletion by selecting the **U** option. The MARKED FOR DELETION message will then be removed from your screen.

0=Exit. When you select the **0** option, the program will return to the Main Menu.

Generating Reports

In addition to producing standard bibliographies, the program offers a number of useful reports. Note: All of the reports will line up properly on 8.5 x ll-inch paper using 15 character-per-inch type. To create any report, select Generate Reports (Option #3) from the Main Menu. The Print Menu will then be displayed, offering you two options:

1   Print entire database.

2. Print selected records.

Print Entire Database

1. If you choose Print Entire Database, the Sort Order Selection Menu will be displayed. Choose the option by which you want the report sorted. Once the sort order is selected, the Report Selection Menu will be displayed. Be sure to select a sort option that is logical for the report you wish to generate. For example, you should probably select the Topic sort order for the Topic report, the Footnote sort order for the Footnote report, the Subject sort order for the Subject report, and the Topic sort order for the Subject within Topic

report. Any sort order may be used with the Summary, Detailed, Abstract, or Bibliography reports.

2. Select the kind of report you want from the Report Selection Menu, which offers the following options:

    Summary report. Contains all fields except Abstract, which is printed in a separate report (see below). The Summary Report prints eight citations per page. (Suggested sort order: any.)

    Detailed report. Presents the same information as the Summary Report, but is displayed exactly as it appears on the screen, two records per page. Use this report when you need space between entries to annotate or edit your entries. (Suggested sort order: any.)

    Abstract report. Prints the abstract for each record. The left side of the report shows the author(s) and title, while the abstract is printed on the right side. If there is no abstract, the report will still list the author(s) and title. (Suggested sort order: any.)

    Bibliography report. Lists the citations according to *The Chicago Manual of Style*. Note: This report automatically adjusts for the differences in book and journal entries. (Suggested sort order: any.)

    Footnote report. Prints out the citations by footnote order. Footnote numbers are listed. (Suggested sort order: only Footnote.)

    Topic report. Prints out citations organized by topic. (Suggested sort order: only Topic.)

    Subject report. Groups together all citations with the same subject, provided they have been input consistently. (Suggested sort order: Subject.)

    Subject within topic report. Prints your citations by subject within topic. For example, all records that have the topic Health Care Cost Reduction would be printed under that topic heading. Within that topic, all records that also have the subject HMO's would be grouped together. Beneath them, all records with the subject Third-Party Reimbursement would be grouped together, and so on. This report automatically starts each topic on a new page. (Suggested sort order: Topic.)

3. Once you have selected the type of report you want to print, a Message screen will prompt you to:

    ```
    Align printer and press enter to continue
    ```

    Make sure your printer is on-line before pressing **<ENTER>**. Otherwise you will get an error message. Retry with your printer on-line. Note: If you are using a version of dBXL earlier than 1.1, you may have to restart from the beginning of the program.

Print Selected Records

This option from the Print Menu allows you to select specific kinds of records to be printed. Take these steps:

1. When you press 2, a Report Criteria Input screen will be displayed. Notice that the screen is identical to the Bibliography Input screen you used to enter and edit records, with the exception that only certain fields are highlighted and some are split into ranges (see below). You can select the records you want to filter from the database by indicating your criteria in the highlighted fields. For example, entering B in the Type field will print all records with B in that field. If you wanted to further refine the list you might specify DRGs in one of the Key Word fields. This will only print out citations that refer to books (assuming that B corresponds to books) and that mention DRGs.

   One caveat: A record must meet *all* your search criteria to pass through the filter. So if you make the selection filter too fine by adding too many criteria, you will probably not print any records at all. Unfortunately, there is no absolute number of criteria above which the filter function defeats itself; each database has its own limits. With a little experimenting, however, you will quickly determine the maximum productive levels of criteria that can be used for your data.

   Note that the key words field is split into four separate fields on the criteria screen, but that on the bibliography input screen you entered the words in one large field. Some of the words you originally entered in the record may be too long to fit into one of the four fields. Don't worry, a match is made on the basis of the letters entered, so you will most likely locate the records you are seeking. If you enter more than one key word in the Report Criteria screen, a record must match *both* words to be included.

   Finally, two fields deserve special attention: Order and Footnote. These fields are displayed as ranges, separated by a dash. They allow you to print a range of records; for example, records numbered 100 through 120, or footnotes 22 through 43. If you want to capture records with all Order or Footnote numbers, leave the fields blank.

   Once you have entered the criteria by which you wish to filter the database, press **CTRL-END**, or press **<ENTER>** in the last highlighted field (publisher). The Sort Order Selection Menu described above will be displayed. Select the order by which you want records to be printed. The program will then look for records that match the criteria you input, and create a report from them.

2. If any records match your criteria, the program will display a Criteria Search Results screen that indicates how many records met your criteria. The Criteria Search Results screen gives you the following options:

   Press P to print. Use this option if you wish to print out the selected records. You will be presented with the Report Selection Menu. The menu will indicate how many records are to be printed, along with criteria you used to select them. The report formats are the same as those used to print the entire database (see below for a description). Note that when reports are printed out after a criteria search, the criteria used will be indicated at the top of the page.

Press S to display on screen. Before you print a report, you may want to view the bibliographic references first to make sure you have retrieved the correct one(s). Or, you may just wish to review the selected records. This option allows you to do either. When you press **S**, the program will display the first citation that met your search criteria, in Scanning Screen format. If more than one citation was found, you can page forward and backward through the selected records by using **F** (forward) and **B** (backward). The principle is the same as that used in the editing process described above.

To view the abstract, press **T** (text). The screen will then be redisplayed with the word *memo* highlighted in the Abstract field. Press **CTRL-PgDn** and the abstract will be displayed. When you are done viewing the abstract, press **ESC** or **CTRL-END**.

After you are finished examining the selected records, press **0** to return to the Report Selection Menu. You can then print the selected records, or return to the Main Menu by pressing **0**.

Using Utilities

The Bibliography Program includes three housekeeping functions. These are accessed from the Utilities Menu, which you used earlier to set up the program. The Utilities Menu is accessed by selecting Option #4 from the Main Menu. The options are described below.

Reindex. Occasionally, you may find that the search routines are not operating correctly. The most probable cause for this is a damaged index. This usually results from illegally exiting the program (see below for the proper exit routine). If this should occur, you must reindex the files by selecting Option #1 from the Utilities Menu. The reindexing option will take a variable period of time depending on the number of records in the file and the type of computer you are using. The reindexing process is initiated as soon as you select Option #1 from the Utilities Menu.

Pack. Packing is the final stage used to delete marked records (see Editing/Viewing/Deleting Citations and Abstract, above). Unlike marking a record, though, packing is irreversible; once a bibliographic citation is packed, it no longer exists. After selecting the pack option, the program will display how many records will be packed, and you will be asked to confirm your choice with a **Y** plus **<ENTER>**. The packing process can take several minutes or longer, since it must update all indexes.

System setup. The Bibliography Program uses the dBXL To Go basic setup options. These are described in Chapter 1.

Note: If you want to delete all records and start with a clean database, you can either recopy the .dbf files from your distribution diskette or use the dBXL Zap command to erase all records. Zap simultaneously deletes and packs all records in your database. To use Zap, make current the directory in which you keep your Bibliography Program files. Start dBXL, and at the command prompt type:

```
use biblio
```

Next, type:

```
zap
```

Zap will ask you to confirm the action with a **Y** or **N**. When you select **Y**, all records will be erased and deleted from your database. After zapping, you must reindex to ensure that your indexes correspond to the program.

> **CAUTION:** Zap is a irrevocable command, and there is no way to recover a zappd file. Therefore, back up your data before zapping it!

Exiting

It is vitally important that you properly exit from the Bibliography Program. Failure to do so may cause file or index damage. While it is often possible to remedy the situation by reindexing, the damage may be permanent, in which case you must start over again by copying the files from your working diskette and re-entering your data, or restoring your database from your most recent backup copy. Given the needless waste of time and the aggravation in reconstructing a database, *always exit by pressing* **0** *in the menu you are working with until you reach the Main Menu.* Pressing **0** at the Main Menu will close all database files and return you to a Sign-Off screen that asks you if you wish to leave the program. Entering **Y** returns you to DOS. Entering **N** returns you to the Main Menu. Note: If you are running an uncompiled program, pressing **X** will return you to the dBXL prompt.

11 Manual For Capital Assets Tracking Program

Features

- Menu driven.
- Password protection.
- Complete system for recording capital assets and determining depreciation and residual value.
- Comprehensive input screen provides fields for all aspects of the asset, including department and budget centers to which it is assigned.
- Two user-defined codes provide flexibility for customizing database.
- Extensive reports show residual value at any time, or cumulative depreciation during the life of an asset.
- Flexible sorting routines.

Contents

Introduction

This program is a complete system for tracking the capital assets of a small business. Each record allows you to input detailed information about the asset, including a user assigned number, the location within the company, the purchase cost and source, and the expected lifespan. The program will automatically calculate the depreciation and residual value. You can use the information to assess the capital asset worth of your business at any time. In addition, the reports can be used for depreciation calculations and intracompany expense reporting purposes.

The system derives additional power from the ability to assign two codes (Asset Codes 1 and 2) to each record. These can be used to tailor the system to your precise reporting needs. The codes can be used to designate specific categories of your choice.

The program offers five types of reports:

1. Summary report. Gives you all data in compact form.

2. Detailed report. Prints out all information as it was entered into the database.

3. Department/budget center summary report. Subtotals residual value of all capital assets for each budget center within a department.

4. Department/budget center detailed report. Gives detailed listing of capital asset values of each budget center and department.

5. Cumulative depreciation report. Gives depreciation values for each department over a user-defined time span.

Depreciation and residual value are calculated with a straight-line depreciation scheme over the life of the asset, using a 365-day year. The residual value can be calculated at any point, and the value is appended to the database.

Cumulative depreciation is calculated between any two user-specified dates. The depreciation period can be entirely within the life of the asset, or overlapping the purchase or the end-of-depreciable-life date. In this way, you can use the cumulative depreciation calculations to show the total depreciation to be charged to a given department or budget center for the period in question without regard to the individual purchase dates or end of depreciable life. The program will automatically calculate the total.

All functions of the Capital Assets Tracking Program are accessed by menus that include instructions on the bottom of the screen. These menus allow you to customize the program report header and printer specifications, establish passwords, scan records, print reports; and update the asset records file using various file utilities and edit functions.

Before using the program, read through this manual and familiarize yourself with all the input, report, and utility functions. You may want to set up a practice capital assets tracking system, using two or three asset records to review the functions of the program. Also, create a backup disk for your database file (Cap.dbf). there's no need to back up your program (.prg), format (.fmt), or report (.frm) files. You can always recopy them from your working diskette. You don't have to back up your index files either, since your program creates them if they aren't found in the directory.

At a minimum, back up your Cap.dbf file each time you add or edit records; the few minutes that the procedure requires will more than offset the time you would need to spend if the entire database had to be recreated. Remember, *no* hardware system is infallible, and it's better to be safe than sorry!

Finally, if you are an experienced dBXL user and wish to modify the program, refer to the Technical Appendix charts and tables. You will find a program tree that lists the calling program hierarchy, a table that describes each index file, and a list of files required to run the program.

Data Entry Keys

After you have input data, you may use the Backspace key to erase your entry (provided that you haven't pressed **<ENTER>**). Alternately, you can use the cursor and Delete/Insert keys to modify your entry. When you do press **<ENTER>**, the cursor will move to the next data input field. If you need to return to a previous entry, use the up cursor key to move the cursor to the desired field. Enter your changes and press **<ENTER>** to move on through the input screen. Note that any errors made during data entry can also be corrected later by means of the Edit option (see below).

Installing and Setting up the Program

Before you begin using the Capital Assets Tracking Program, you will have to install and set it up. General instructions for installation and setup are in Chapter 1.

Starting the Program

The easiest way to start the Capital Assets Tracking Program is to create a batch file. You can also start the program manually by typing:

```
do cap
```

after starting dBXL (see Chapter 1 for specifics of both startup techniques).

Regardless of how you begin the Capital Assets Tracking Program, you will first see the dBXL copyright and license notice. The screen will then display the message "Creating indexes, please wait." This process may require a few seconds, but only occurs the first time you run the program after installation. The Capital Assets Tracking Program Main Menu will then appear.

Adding a Capital Asset Record

All data is entered into the program through the Asset Input screen. To call up the Asset Input screen, select Option #1, Add Records, from the Main Menu. The Asset Input screen consists of three major sections:

Asset information section. Provides fields for basic information about the identification of the asset and its location.

Coding information section. Describes the department and the budget center to which the asset is assigned, and user-defined codes.

Purchase/depreciation section. Contains asset cost information and calculates residual value. Also provides fields for entering replacement costs.

Asset Information Section

When you select Add Records from the Main Menu, the cursor will move through the following sequence of fields each time you press <ENTER>:

Item. Enter the name or model number of the asset. Be consistent in the way you enter data; if you enter IBM PC for some records and IBM-PC (with a hyphen) for others, you will have difficulty searching for all your IBM PC's. Further, they may not be grouped together on reports. Bear in mind that punctuation characters and spaces count as bona fide data; I.B.M. (with periods) is treated differently than IBM.

Description. Use this field to enter a brief description of the item.

Location. This field can be used to describe where the asset is located within a particular site (e.g., 3rd floor—personnel). It can also be used to designate a facility within a multisite company (e.g., Westboro, 8th floor, Cafe). The Location field can be sorted, so you must be consistent when you enter data.

Asset #. You can assign an alphanumeric character of up to 15 digits.

Serial #. Enter any alphanumeric combination, up to 15 digits.

Coding Information Section

Department. Enter the department name or code to which the asset is assigned. Again, consistency is vitally important if the program is to properly search for records and list records with the same departments together on reports. In general, simple codes are recommended over names, as they minimize confusion when more than one operator is using the computer. Keep a list of codes by the computer for all operators to use, and you will minimize the risks of inconsistent entries.

Budget center. If your company explicitly designates budget centers, enter the name or code in this field. Again, consistency is vitally important, and codes are recommended over names. Add budget centers to the list kept by the computer.

Asset codes 1 and 2. Use these fields to enter any codes of your choice. For example, you might want to use the codes to designate types of equipment: 001 might be furniture, 002 might be data processing equipment, 003 might be vehicles. You could further break down the codes so that 001D represents desks, 002C represents computers, and 003A stands for autos. The second code could be used to further refine the categories or designate other features.

Regardless of the coding system you develop, consistency is the key to success. For that reason, we recommend using simple codes and keeping a code list by the computer so users don't invent them on the fly.

Purchase/Depreciation Section

This section is divided into two subsections. The first provides purchase information that is used to calculate residual values and replacement costs.

PURCHASE INFORMATION

Source. Enter the company from which the asset was purchased.

Cost. Enter the asset's purchase price.

Date. Enter the date on which the asset was purchased.

Life. Enter the lifetime of the asset, in years.

DEPRECIATION INFORMATION

Residual value. This is a calculated field. Note: Because of the structure of the program, calculations are made *after* the record has been appended to the database. You can view the calculation by using the program's edit function (see below) or by generating a report (see below).

Calculation date. This is the date that was used to calculate the most recent residual value. Typically this will be calculated for the end of the fiscal year, but can be set for any specific date during the residual recalculation process (see below).

Replacement cost. Use this field to enter the estimated cost of replacing the asset.

Estimate date. Enter the date at which the replacement cost was estimated.

Adding Another Asset Record

When you press **<ENTER>** while the cursor is in the Estimate Date field, or press **CTRL-END** elsewhere during data input, the record will be included in the database. A prompt at the bottom of the screen will then ask if you want to add another record. To accept the default **Y** and continue adding records, press **<ENTER>**. If you enter **N**, the program will return to the Main Menu. At a minimum, an asset number or name must be entered for a record to be valid.

Editing/Viewing/Deleting Records

The Scan Function

To recall a previously created asset record, select the Edit/Delete Records option from the Main Menu (Option #2). This will display various criteria by which you can scan for records in the database.

Scanning is used to search for a record or group of records, and then to display them on the screen. It is useful for two purposes. First, it will enable you to pinpoint a specific record for viewing, editing, or deleting, as explained below. Second, you can locate a group of records and display them one by one for editing or deletion.

One way to think of the second scan function is to imagine the records on a track. When you scan for, say, all assets records with the department code AP, the program will find the first record that has that designation in the Department field. You can view the rest of the records, one after another, forward and backward (by pressing **F** and **B**, see editing options, below). The records will appear alphabetically in the order determined by the criteria you selected. If you enter a blank scan criteria and press **<ENTER>** or **ESC**, the program will display the first record in the database, according to the criteria you selected.

Note: You can use contractions of the name you are seeking and the program will find the first record matching the contractions. For example, if you only enter C for a scan by name, the program will display the first record starting with the letter C.

Scanning Procedures

The following process is identical for each scan option:

1. Select the field on which you want to scan for records. The Scanning Criteria Input screen will then be displayed. Enter the appropriate information. Be as specific as possible, or else you may not locate the asset record(s) you are seeking.

2. If any records match the word(s), contraction(s), or number(s) you entered, the record you are seeking will be displayed in Scanning Screen format. You can then use the options described below to edit, view, or delete the information. If more than one record matches the name or word you entered (e.g., 30 records with department code 001), the program will display the first one entered. If you enter a contraction, the order is determined by the full length of the field.

3. If no asset records in the database match the word(s) or number(s) entered in the Scanning Criteria Input screen, the program will display the following message:

```
No records meet your criteria
Press any key to continue
```

Scanning Options

Once you have located the desired asset records, you can use any of the functions listed at the bottom of the Scanning screen.

F=Forward, B=Backward. Each time your press **F**, you will browse forward from one asset record to another. To move backward through the file, press **B**. The program will move backward one record each time the **B** key is pressed. If you try to scan past the end of the file (the record most recently input), or the beginning of the file (the first record entered), the program will beep and remain on the last or first record.

E = Edit. Once you have located an asset record for editing through the Scan option, select item **E** and the program will then enter full screen edit mode. Each field will be highlighted on the screen, just as it was during initial data entry. You can move from highlighted field to highlighted field by using the cursor or pressing **<ENTER>.** Each time you press **<ENTER>,** the cursor will advance one field. Make your changes in a field using the Backspace, Insert, and Delete keys. The editing process is ended by pressing **CTRL-END** in any field, or by pressing **<ENTER>** in the last field, Estimate Date. Either action will save the information to disk. You can exit without saving the changes to disk by pressing the **ESC** key. Note: The Residual Value field can only be recalculated by selecting Option #4 from the Main Menu.

D = Delete. Deletion with the Capital Asset Tracking Program is a two-step process. First, press **D** to mark the record for deletion. MARKED FOR DELETION will appear at the bottom of the record. Although a record is marked for deletion, it is not actually erased from the database until you use the Pack function, which is accessed from the Utilities Menu (see below). Records may remain in the marked state indefinitely. Even when you exit the program and return at a later date, records slated for deletion will still be marked.

U = Undelete. If you decide that you do not want to delete a marked record and you haven't used the Pack function yet (see Using Utilities), you can unmark the record by selecting the **U** option. The MARKED FOR DELETION message will then be removed from the record.

0 = Exit. When you select the **0** option, the program will return to the Main Menu.

Generating Reports

CAUTION: Make sure that you recalculate the residual value (see Option #4, Main Menu) before running a report; otherwise, your report totals will be incorrect.

The Capital Assets Tracking Program uses several report formats and organizational schemes to print your asset data. All the reports will line up properly on 8.5 x 11-inch paper using condensed (15 characters per inch) type. To create any of the reports, select the Generate Reports option (#3) from the Main Menu. The Print Menu will then be displayed, offering you two options:

1. Print entire database.

2. Print selected records.

Print Entire Database

Take the following steps to print all the records you have entered:

1. When you choose Print Entire Database from the Print Menu, a Sort Order Selection Menu will be displayed. Choose the option by which you want the report sorted.

2. Once the sort order is selected, the Report Selection Menu will be displayed (see below for descriptions). Be sure to select a sort option that is logical for the report you wish to generate. For example, you should probably select the Department sort order for the Department/Budget Report; otherwise, the organization of the report may be confusing.

3 Select the kind of report you want from the Report Selection Menu, which offers the following options:

Summary report. Contains all fields, organized in compact form. The Summary report prints eight asset records per page. (Suggested sort order: any.)

Detailed report. Presents the same information as the summary report, but displayed exactly as it appears on the screen, two per page. Use this report when you need space between entries to annotate or edit your entries. (Suggested sort order: any.)

Department/budget summary report. Prints total residual value and replacement costs for budget centers within departments. No detail information is included in the report. (Suggested sort order: dept.)

Department/budget data report. Subtotals assets by budget center within department, as Summary report does, but shows each asset record as a detail line item. (Suggested sort order: dept.)

Cumulative depreciation report. Prints out the cumulative depreciation of each asset for a user-defined period of time. When you select this option, you will be prompted to enter starting and ending dates, and to confirm your choice before the report is generated. (Suggested sort order: any.)

Once you have selected the type of report you want to print, a Message screen will prompt you to:

```
Align printer and press enter to continue
```

Make sure your printer is on-line before pressing **<ENTER>**. Otherwise you will get an error message. Retry with your printer on line.

Print Selected Records

This option from the Print Menu allows you to select specific kinds of records to be printed. Take the following steps:

1. When you press **2**, the Report Criteria Input screen will be displayed. Notice that the screen is identical to the input screen you used to enter records, except that only certain fields are highlighted, and some are expanded into ranges (see below). You can select the records you want to filter from the database by indicating your criteria in the highlighted fields. For example, entering 00lD in Asset Code 1 will print all records with 00lD in that field. If you wanted to further refine the list, you might also specify department code AP. This will only output records that match the criteria in *both* fields. If you enter a contraction of a code you can make the test more general. For example, if you enter 001 in the Asset Code 1 field, you would include both 00lD and 00lE. By creating hierarchical codes, you can greatly increase the power of the record selection logic.

   One caveat: To pass through the filter, a record must meet *all* your search criteria. So if you make the selection filter too fine by adding too many criteria, you will probably not print any records at all. Unfortunately, there is no absolute number of criteria above which the filter function defeats itself; each database has its own limits. With a little experimentation, however, you will quickly determine the maximum productive levels of criteria that can be used for your data.

   Note that the Residual Value and Acquisition Date fields in the Report Criteria Input Screen are split into ranges with an upper and lower limit. This allows you to locate groups of assets. For example, you might want to locate all assets purchased between 12/31/84 and 12/31/86, or all items with residual values between $5,000 and $10,000. If you want to search for a specific number rather than a range in a particular field, enter the number as both the upper and lower limits. Say you want to find all assets purchased on December 31, 1986. Enter 12/31/86 in both highlighted date fields. The same holds true for the Residual Value fields.

   Once you have entered the criteria by which you wish to filter the database, press **CTRL-END**, or press **<ENTER>** in the last highlighted field (Residual Value). The Sort Order Selection Menu described above will be displayed. Select the order by which you want records to be printed. The program will then look for records that match the criteria you input, and create a report from them.

2. If any records match your criteria, the program will display the Criteria Search Results screen, which indicates how many records met your criteria. The Criteria Search Results screen gives you the following options, in addition to pressing **ESC** to return to the Main Menu:

Press **P** *to print*. Use this option if you wish to print out the selected records. You will be presented with the Report Selection Menu. The menu will indicate how many records are to be printed, along with the criteria you used to select them. The report formats are the same as those used to print the entire database (see above for a description). Note that when reports are printed out after a criteria search, the criteria used will be indicated at the top of the page.

Press **S** *to display on screen*. Before you print a report, you may want to view the asset records to make sure you have retrieved the correct one(s). Or, you may just wish to review the selected records on the screen. This option allows you to do either. When you press S, the program will display the first record that met your search criteria, in Scanning Screen format. If more than one asset was found, you can page forward and backward through the selected records by using **F** (forward) and **B** (backward). The principle is the same as that used in the editing process described above.

After you have finished examining the selected records, press **0** to return to the Report Selection Menu. You can then print the selected records, or return to the Main Menu by pressing **0**.

3. If no records are located, the program displays the message:

```
No records meet your criteria
Press any key to continue
```

Recalculating Residual Values

The Capital Assets Tracking Program is structured so that recalculating residual values is a user-initiated task. The reason is that most companies require residual value calculations as of a certain date, usually the end of the month or year. When you select Option #4 from the Main Menu, the program will display a Residual Value Calculation screen. This screen prompts you to enter the date for which you would like the program to recalculate the residual value. Enter and confirm the date, and the calculation will be made. If you wish to edit the date before the program recalculates the values, enter **N** at the confirmation prompt, and the cursor will move to the beginning of the date field again.

Using Utilities

The Capital Assets Tracking Program includes four housekeeping functions. These are accessed from the Utilities Menu, which you used earlier to set up the program. The Utilities Menu is accessed by selecting Option #5 from the Main Menu. The options are described below.

Reindex. Occasionally, you may find that the search routines are not operating correctly. The most probable cause for this is a damaged index. This usually results from illegally exiting the program (see below for the proper exit routine). If this should occur, you must reindex the files by selecting Option #1 from the Utilities Menu. The reindexing option will take a variable period of time depending on the number of records in the file or the computer you are using.

Pack. Packing is the final stage used to delete marked records (refer to Editing/Viewing/Deleting Records, above). Unlike marking a record, though, packing is an irreversible action; once an asset record is packed, it no longer exists. After selecting the pack option, the program will display how many records will be packed, and you will be asked to confirm your choice with a **Y** plus **<ENTER>**. The packing process can take several minutes or longer, since it must update all indexes.

Delete selected records. While the edit functions discussed earlier allow you to delete records one by one using the marking/packing functions, this option allows you to quickly delete groups of records. When you select Option #3 from the Utilities Menu, a submenu will be displayed, offering you four deletion choices. When you select any of the deletion options, an input screen will be displayed and will prompt you to specify what kinds of records are to be deleted. For example, when you choose Option #1, the input screen will provide a field for you to enter a specific department name or code. (This is another good reason to use codes rather than names; any records that have a department name that is inconsistent with the name that you enter into the input screen will not be deleted.)

Once you have entered a specific name or code to be deleted, the program will indicate how many records will be erased from the database and ask you to confirm your choice. Be certain that you wish to proceed since this routine both deletes and packs the database; once the records are deleted, there is no way to retrieve them! Before using the delete functions, you would be well advised to back up your .dbf files, just in case you change your mind or discover that certain records are still needed.

If no records in the database meet your criteria, the program will indicate that no records were deleted, and prompt you to press a key to continue. You will then return to the Delete Selected Records Menu (or Main Menu).

System setup. The Capital Assets Tracking Program uses the dBXL To Go setup options described in Chapter 1.

Note: If you want to delete all records and start with a clean database, you can either recopy the .dbf files from your distribution diskette or use the dBXL Zap command to erase all records. Zap simultaneously deletes and packs all records in your database. To use Zap, make the directory in which you keep your Capital Assets Tracking Program files current. Start dBXL, and at the command prompt type:

```
use cap
```

Next, type:

```
zap
```

dBXL will ask you to confirm the action with a **Y** or N. When you select **Y**, all records will be erased and deleted from your database. After zapping, you must reindex to ensure that your indexes correspond to the program.

> **CAUTION**: Zap is irrevocable; there is no way to recover a zapped file. Therefore, back up your data before zapping it!

Exiting

It is vitally important that you exit properly from the Capital Assets Tracking Program. Failure to do so may cause file or index damage. While it is often possible to remedy the situation by reindexing, the damage may be permanent, in which case you must start over again by copying the files from your working diskette and re-entering your data, or restoring your database from your most recent backup copy. Given the needless waste of time and the aggravation in reconstructing a database, *always exit by pressing* **0** *in the menu you are working with until you reach the Main Menu.* Pressing **0** at the Main Menu will close all database files and return you to a Sign-Off screen that asks you if you wish to leave the program. Entering **Y** returns you to DOS. Entering **N** returns you to the Main Menu. Note: If you are running an uncompiled program, pressing **X** will return you to the dBXL prompt.

12 Utilities

Contents

1. and 2. Password Encryption/Decrytion Systems

Description

The password protection utility is a gateway to a calling program. It protects access to a .prg file by interrupting the path for a password test, and then either allows the user to continue, or diverts the system back to DOS. The utility is designed to prevent casual users from accidentally accessing certain programs or viewing confidential data. The system uses screen attributes to blank the actual password as it is input, so that it can't be viewed on the screen.

Note that the password utilities do NOT encrypt the .dbf files or prevent access to them; they merely prevent use of the calling program. To make the utility most effective, compile your program using WordTech Systems, Inc's. Quicksilver compiler.

Files

UTPW.PRG: Creates password and interrupts calling program.
UTPW.DBF: Stores the passwords.

UTECRYPT.PRG: Takes an English language ASCII string and converts it into virtually indecipherable higher order ASCII characters.

UTDCRYPT.PRG: Reverses utecrypt.prg.

Logic

UTPW.PRG uses the UTECRYPT program to encrypt a user-defined password and store it in the UTPW.DBF file. Subsequent passes through the program will automatically check the inputted password against the existing UTPW.DBF file. Three outcomes are possible:

1. It finds an acceptable match. UTPW then passes control back to the calling program.

2. It determines that the input string is the master password. The program then brings up the Master Password Maintenance Menu. The master password maintenance routine allows you to assign passwords to other uses, edit existing passwords, delete passwords from the system, or output to screen a list of all passwords in the database.

3. A match is not found. UTPW then allows the user to re-input the password. If a match still isn't found, the calling program is terminated, and the system returns to DOS.

Programming Notes

The password system is designed to work with the dBXL Plus To Go programs in this book, and incorporates the same screen design and layout features. The format, ID labels, and variables are set by a program called UTID.PRG. You can, however, easily use the password system without UTID.PRG; if UTPW.PRG does not find the ID variables, it substitutes a blank. The calling syntax for UTPW.PRG is do UTPN. The program should be placed in the beginning of a .PRG file after you set the environment.

ENCRYPTION/DECRYPTION ROUTINES

UTPW calls UTECRYPT and UTDCRYPT with a master encryption code labeled mpass=" GRIZ". This can be changed to any alphanumeric form using up to six characters to make your password unique. UTECRYPT encrypts an ASCII character string by character substitution using two levels of encryption. When the encryption program is called, the user provides a master encryption code. Second, each copy of encrypt and decrypt has the opportunity to set a unique increment code (a number between one and one hundred) that will make the UTECRYPT/UTDCRYPT program pair unique.

> **WARNING!** For the encrypt and decrypt pair to work together, the increment in the actual .prg files must be identical, and the master encryption code used when calling the encryption routine must be the same.

The syntax for UTECRYPT and UTDCRYPT are as follows:

```
do utecrypt with " [ X ] ", " [ Y ] "
```

where [X] is the word to be encrypted, and [Y] is the master encryption code. The encrypted version of the word is returned in the public variable named CRYPT, which is declared public by the UTECRYPT/UTDCRYPT program. Note that you can use multiple versions of UTPW.PRG to create multiple levels of password protection. For example, you could have one level that allows access to the program, say for data entry or editing, and another level for access to the report generator. To do so, however, you must change the name of the UTPW.DBF file and its reference in UTPW.PRG, since two identically named .DBF files cannot share the same program at the same time. You must also change the master encryption code for each level.

3. and 4. Time Bomb and Demo

Description

Time Bomb is used to protect custom applications where a fee for programming services is due after completion. Should a client refuse to pay the bill by a specified date, the program will cease to function. You then have recourse for extracting payment. If your invoice is paid on time, send your client an updated copy of the program—no one need ever know the utility is in place (see Programming Notes, below, for more strategic suggestions).

Demo protects demonstration programs by setting a limit to the number of records that can be entered into the database. If the record count is exceeded, the program no longer functions. Both utilities display a user-definable message when the deactivation levels have been reached.

Files

UTTB.PRG: Checks the system date against a user-specified time period.

UTDEMO.PRG: Checks record count against a user-defined record limit.

Logic

Both utilities compare a user specified value (date, UTTB.PRG or record count, UTDEMO). When the value has been reached, they display a warning message and return the system to DOS.

Programming Note

To incorporate either utility into your programs, you must first use MODIFY COMMAND to insert three fields.

Time Bomb (UTTB.PRG)

1. Insert the cutoff date specified as mtbdate=ctod(" // ").

2   Contact name = " [X] " where [X] is the name of the person who should be contacted if time bomb is detonated. This name appears on the warning message.

3. Tele = " [X] " where [X] is the telephone number of the contact. This also appears on the warning message.

Then invoke the program with:

```
do uttb
```

Demo (UTDEMO.PRG)

1. Insert the record limit, above which the program will not process the data and returns to DOS. The code is mdemo count="[X]", where [X] is the number of allowable records.

2. Contact name (same as TIME BOMB)

3. Tele (same as TIME BOMB)

Then invoke the program with:

```
do utdemo
```

If you want to change the overall warning message, which says:

```
Demonstration Time Limit Exceeded
Contact:          Telephone:
for additional information
```

use MODI COMM and enter a new one of your choice.

TIME BOMB can be placed anywhere in the calling program. In the case of DEMO, however, you must *use* the file you want to test *before* you call the test routine.

To be effective, both programs should be compiled with a third-party compiler such as Quicksilver compiler WordTech Systems. As a precaution against anyone circumventing Time Bomb, make sure that the system date occurs on all printouts and screens, as a disincentive for continually changing the system date. Finally, as an ultimate precaution, you can use both Time Bomb and Demo in conjunction, so that the program freezes either at a specified date or record count, whichever comes first.

5. Reindex

Description

The Reindex utility gives the user a window on the reindexing process by providing an estimated time required to reindex a file. It then prompts the user whether or not to continue the operation. If an affirmative response is given, the utility updates all indexes. If not, control returns to the calling program.

Files

UTREDEX.PRG: Computes reindexing time and carries out reindex function.

Logic

The Reindex utility assumes the standard dBXL To Go screen format. If you wish to use another format, make the changes through MODI COMM. Reindex time calculation is based on an average of 300 records/minute. Note that this will greatly vary depending on (1) how many indexes you have; (2) the complexity of the index structure; and (3) the type of computer you are using. Before installing this utility in an application, we recommend setting up your own benchmark tests and, if necessary, changing the calculation basis by altering the divisor in the .prg file from 300 to the appropriate number.

Programming Note

The syntax for the utility is as follows:

```
do utredex with "file name", "index name(s)"
```

With multiple indexes, be sure to separate index names with commas. The utility will reindex each one.

6. Pack

Description

The Pack utility computes the number of records that will be deleted and packed, and prompts the user to confirm whether or not to continue the function. Control returns to the calling program if the user does not wish to continue the packing operation.

Files

UTPACK.PRG: Computes number of records to be packed, then completes deletion and packing functions.

Logic

The Pack utility assumes the standard dBXL To Go screen format. If you wish to use another format, make the changes through MODI COMM.

When the Pack utility is run, it displays the message:

```
X out of Y records will be permanently deleted.
Are you sure you want to pack them (Y/N)?
```

Programming Note

The syntax for the utility is as follows:

```
do utpack with "file name","index name(s)"
```

With multiple indexes, be sure to separate the index names with commas.

7. Blank Delete

Description

This utility removes blank records from your database. Before cleaning the database, UTBLKDEL calculates how many records will be deleted, displays the result, and asks the user for a confirmation before continuing the process.

Files

UTBLKDEL.PRG: Tests for specified fields as being blank, then deletes and packs.

Logic

UTBLKDEL scans the database for records with the specified field string equal to blank. It notifies the user of the results of continuing; if the user confirms deletion, it deletes the blank records and packs the database.

Programming Notes

The syntax for UTBLKDEL is:

```
do utblkdel with "file name", "index name(s)",
"test field string"
```

The index names must be separated by commas. The test field string is a concatenation of the (character) fields you want to test (e.g., fieldl + field2 + field3).

> **WARNING**: Do not concatenate numeric or date fields. Numeric data will be converted to a 0, which is not considered blank. Dates will also be converted to characters (the slashes / / remaining in the field), and will not be treated as blanks either.

8. Printer Control

Description

These utilities set the print size by transmitting the required ASCII control character to the printer. They allow you to change printer setup strings (even lengthy strings for laser printers) in any subroutine by means of public variables.

Files

UTCOMP.PRG: Sets printer to compressed print type (15 characters per inch).

UTNORM.PRG: Sets printer to normal print type (10 characters per inch).

Logic

Each utility exports ASCII characters through the "?? CHR (char string)" function. The character string is initiated as a public variable prior to calling either .prg.

Programming Note

You must set NORMAL and COMPRESS as public variables to the appropriate numeric value as characters prior to calling UTCOMP or UTNORM. The syntax is:

```
do utnorm
```

or

```
do utcomp
```

Note: As provided, UTNORM and UTCOMP work in conjunction with the dBXL To Go UTID program. If you do not use UTID, you must set them to the appropriate strings prior to calling UTCOMP and UTNORM.

9. Printer Test

Description

These utilities test for printer readiness, and warn the user to put the printer on-line before a report is printed. While current versions of dBXL test for printer readiness, not all compilers support the built-in function. Older versions of dBXL also do not test for printer readiness. If the program does detect an error, it will display a message to the user, and allow four retries. On the fifth, it will return to DOS.

Files

UTPRNTES.PRG: Tests for proper on-line status of printer.
UTPRNERR.PRG: Displays error message.

Logic

The Printer Test uses the on-error function of dBXL to detect a printer error and redirect the system to display a message. The counter checks for five cycles before returning the system to DOS.

Programming Note

The syntax for UTPRNTES is:

```
do utprntes
```

UTPRNTES should be executed before a Report Form line or Set Device to Print command. UTPRNERR is called from UTPRNTES.

10. Program Listing

Description

PRGPRN is a DOS batch file that creates and prints a directory of all .prg and .fmt files in the current directory. The file's name, extension, size, and dates are sorted alphabetically and subsequently printed in total. An eject command is issued after each file. Note: PRGPRN must be used with DOS 3.0 or higher.

Files

PRGPRN.BAT: Creates a list of all .PRG and .FMT files in the current directory and prints them.

EJECT: Issues a page eject between program listings.

Logic

The utility uses a DOS batch file to copy a sorted directory to a temporary file. It then prints the file and issues an eject. The core of the batch file takes the form of:

```
for %%F in ( * . prg ) do copy %%F+eject LPT1:
```

which translates to English as: for each member in the set "*.prg," the batch file copies that member plus a concatenated eject to LPT1: . The same holds for .fmt files.

Programming Note

Both PRGPRN and EJECT must be placed in each directory where your dBXL fields are located; the utility does not recognize path names. Execution is done at the DOS prompt by typing PRGPRN.

Note: Before invoking PRGPRN, be sure to set your left margin for three-hole binding if you intend to place the printouts in a notebook. Also, if possible set your perforation skip to avoid type being lost between pages.

Appendix A
Customizing dBXL To Go Programs

Introduction

The key to customizing an application program is to determine which elements are currently suited to your needs and which need to be altered. If more than 30 percent of the existing application needs to be altered, you will probably be better off starting from scratch.

Once you have determined that altering an existing program is the best alternative, there are several steps you must follow to ensure that the revised program performs as anticipated. Depending on the significance of the proposed change relative to the overall system, you will first have to perform some background research. For example, if you only propose to add reports or fields that do not affect the indexes or program files, you need not be overly concerned about the interrelationships of the existing code. If, on the other hand, you propose to delete sections or change the structure of indexes, you must ensure that you do not adversely affect other sections of the code that are dependent on the area of proposed change. The following discussion will give you some general guidelines for modifying dBXL To Go Programs.

Changing Reports

The most common alteration of a software program is a change in the format of the reports. This is easily accomplished with many dBXL To Go programs (with the exception of some of the custom full-screen reports and reports with complex calculated fields), since most of the reports were created using the dBXL MODIFY REPORT command. Reports created through dBXL have the .FRM extension.

The steps to alter a report are:

1. Identify the name of the report file you wish to alter. The easiest way to do this is to list the report menu and its associated subprograms and calling routines (see Program Trees for the program in question). You will have to follow the logic down to the point where it calls for a report with the format REPORT FORM [X], where [X] represents the name of the report. Be sure that you have distinguished between the various report formats that may be used for output to the screen or printer and detailed or summary reporting. Once you are certain that you have identified the correct report format, you can continue the process.

2. Make a copy of the x.frm file and its supporting .prg, .dbf, and .ndx files to a test disk or directory. Make this disk or directory the dBXL default directory.

3. Boot up dBXL, making sure that the report file is still in the default directory.

4. At the Command prompt, enter the dBXL command MODIFY REPORT [X] (MODI REPO [X] for short) and press <ENTER>.

5. Follow the pulldown menus to modify the report as desired. See your dBXL manual for detailed description of the MODIFY REPORT command.

6. Save the report with the modifications.

7. Test the new version to be certain you have made the desired changes, and that in doing so you have not made any alterations that cause the report to fail. Continue to modify and test the report on the test disk or directory.

8. If you copy the new report back to your operational disk, you will overwrite the original report format. Even if you don't intend to use the original report, it is valuable for archival purposes and as a starting point for further modifications. To preserve the original report, rename it with another extension (e.g., [X].ARC). Copy the new version from your test disk and try it. If you are satisfied, you have finished the modification process.

9. Periodically check your operations disk for old .ARC files that you can safely delete. It is good practice to wait until new reports are proven in operation before deleting .ARC files.

Adding Reports

To add a report, you must perform three separate tasks:

1. Create the report format.

2. Add the calling sequence to the report program, and

3. Create a search and selection program to determine which records are to be included in your new report.

Creating the Report Format

1. Determine an appropriate name for the new report format, keeping in mind the naming convention of starting all files with the prefix of the calling programs (e.g., WARE, CAP, TRAV, etc.). This will make it easier to copy files in groups and place them in their proper directories.

2. Copy the programs and test data to a test disk or directory.

3. Boot up dBXL using a test disk or directory as the default directory.

4. Enter the command MODIFY REPORT (or MODI REPO) [X] where [X] is the selected report format name.

5. Follow the dBXL manual for a detailed description of how to create reports using the pulldown menus.

NOTE 1. To include memory variables in your reports, you must first declare them public before trying to modify the report. This is necessary because dBXL checks to see if the variable exists before allowing you to include it in a report.

NOTE 2. To produce multiline reports, you can force the report generator to wrap a field onto more than one line by setting the field width on the report to less than the length of the field. By concatenating several fields together and adding spaces, you can force them to appear in a column. Be careful of trimmed fields and blank field suppression when trying to use this feature.

Adding the Calling Sequence

You must add the new report to the menu and its calling routine. To add to the menu, you must MODIFY COMMAND [X]REP.PRG where [X] refers to the file prefix (e.g., ADDR for Address Book Program files, INV for Invoice Program). Simply edit the menu section of this .prg file to add the new choice. If the reports program already has nine numerical choices, it will accept letter choices as well to permit additions. Edit the CASE section of the report program to add the search and selection program used to select records for the new report.

Creating a Search and Selection Program

1. Copy one of the existing report search and selection programs to a new program name. Select the one that most closely matches the logic you wish to employ in your new report. For example, if you want to include all records of a particular type between two invoice dates, you may want to copy a report program that uses this logic. Review the different reports available and determine their names by matching the menu choice to the CASE section of the program you are modeling. Once you have made a copy of your selection to the newly named .prg file, you can edit it with MODIFY COMMAND [X] where [X] is the new file name.

    CAUTION: As mentioned earlier in this book, if you modify a .prg program, you cannot use the dBXL text editor for files greater than 5K. Otherwise, you might truncate and damage the program you are modifying. For files greater than 5K, you must use a word processor capable of handling ASCII text.

2. After you have changed the selection or searching criteria, be sure to double check the index choice, as this will affect the sequence used in the report. If this needs to be changed, be sure to do so at this time.

Testing Your New Report

1. It is a good practice to develop and maintain a test database that fully exercises the logic of your report as well as testing it on your real data.

2. When you are certain that the report fulfills your expectations, test several of the other reports and systems to ensure that you have not accidentally affected them (which is unlikely in the creation of a new report).

3. When you are certain that you are ready to copy your new report and program back to your operational disk or directory, back up your original. After backing up, you can copy the new version of the new report to your operational disk or directory.

Appendix B
Using dBXL To Go Programs with Laser Printers

As described in Chapter 1, the Compressed and Normal Print setup fields can each be up to 250 characters, which is more than adequate for the escape sequences used with the HP Laser-Jet and other laser printers. To enter an escape sequence, first translate the escape codes into ASCII decimal format. (See dBXL Reference Manual: Appendix D.)

For example, the HP LaserJet escape sequence for the Line Printer font on Cartridge C is:

^{E}C&10O^{E}C(0U^{E}C(s0p16.66h8.5v0s0b0T

This sequence translates into the following ASCII decimal codes:

^{E}C	= 027	6	= 054
&	= 038	h	= 104
l	= 108	8	= 056
0	= 048	.	= 046
O	= 079	5	= 053
(	= 040	v	= 118
s	= 115	b	= 098
p	= 112	T	= 084
1	= 049	U	= 085

The proper way to input the above HP LaserJet escape sequence would thus be:

027 038 108 048 079 027 040 048 085 027 040 115 048 112 049 054
046 054 054 104 056 046 053 118 048 115 048 098 048 084

Enter each set, separated by a space. Since the input screen only allows you to view 20 characters at a time, your entries will scroll to the left. Use the left and right cursor arrows to scroll backward or forward to view or edit the codes already entered.

It is easy to make a mistake, so you must be very careful when entering the codes (upper and lower case have different values. Also you must distinguish zero from upper case "O", and the number one from the letter "1"). Here are some suggestions for minimizing mistakes and troubleshooting problems:

1. Don't enter codes on the fly from an ASCII table. Write the translation, as above, before sitting down at the computer.

2. If possible, have another person read the codes to you. Alternately, read them back to someone else for verification.

Appendix C
Technical Specifications

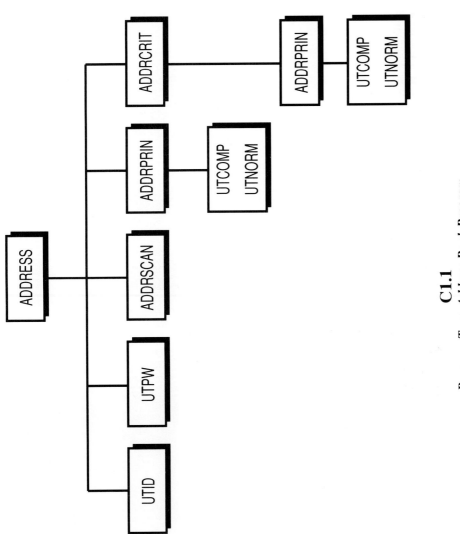

C1.1
Program Tree: Address Book Program

C1.2

Required Files: Address Book Program

Database (.DBF)	Program (.PRG)
ADDRESS	ADDRESS
UTID	ADDRCRIT
UTPW	ADDRPRIN
	ADDRSCAN
	UTCOMP
Format (.FMT)	UTDCRYPT
	UTECRYPT
ADDRDISP	UTEXIT
ADDREDIT	UTFACE
ADDRINP	UTID
	UTNORM
	UTPACK
Report (.FRM)	UTPW
	UTREDEX
ADDRDETL	
ADDRTELE	
Label (.LBL)	
ADDRLABL	
ADDRLARG	
ADDRSMAL	

C1.3

Indexed and Required Fields: Address Book Program

Indexes	*Required Input Field*
– Last Name + First Name	Last Name
– Company + Last Name	Company

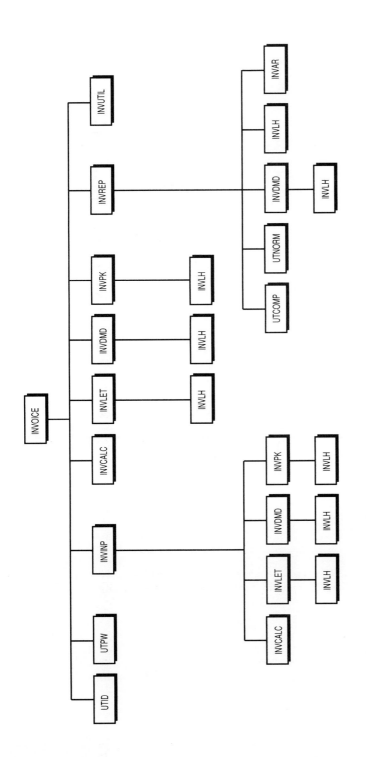

C2.1

Program Tree: Invoice Program

C2.2

Required Files: Invoice Program.

Datebase (.DBF)	Programs (.PRG)
INVARCH	INVINP
INVOICE	INVOICE
UTID	INVREP
UTPW	INVPROC*
	Consists of:
Format (.FMT)	—INVAR
	—INVARCH
INVDISP	—INVCALC
INVED	—INVDMD
INVED2	—INVLET
INVINP	—INVLH
	—INVPK
	—INSCAN
	—INVUTIL
	—INVFIND
	—INVAFC
	—INVNSC
Report (.FRM)	
	UTCOMP
INVDELI	UTCCRYPT
INVLALL	UTECRYPT
INVLSCRC	UTEXIT
INVSDET	UTFACE
INVSSCR	UTID
INVSSUM	UTNORM
INVTAX	UTPACK
INVTAXS	UTPW
Memory (.MEM)	
INVMEM	

* INVPROC.PRG is a procedure file that contains the files listed beneath it. The procedure file is used to save space and boost program speed.

C2.3

Indexed and Required Fields: Invoice Program.

Indexes	*Required Fields*
- Broker+Date	Last Name
- Invoice #	Quantity of
- Customer Last Name	Product A
- First three characters of	
the First Name and Last	
- Name	

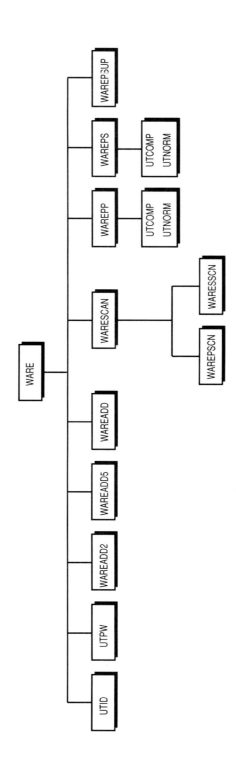

C3.1
Program Tree: Dynamic Inventory
Management Program

C3.2

Required Files: Dynamic Inventory Management Program

Database (.DBF)	Program (.PRG)
WAREBUY	WARE
WARECLNT	WAREPP
WAREPART	WAREPS
WARESALE	WAREPSUP
WARESUPL	WAREPROC*
UTID	Consists of:
UTPW	—WAREADD
	—WAREADD2
	—WAREADD5
Format (.FMT)	—WAREPSCN
	—WARESCAN
WAREBDIS	—WARESSCN
WAREBED	
WARECDIS	UTCOMP
WARECED	UTDCRYPT
WARECINP	UTECRYPT
WARELDIS	UTEXIT
WARELED	UTFACE
WAREPDIS	UTID
WAREPED	UTNORM
WAREPINP	UTPACK
WARESDIS	UTPW
WARESED	
WARESINP	

Report (.FRM)

WAREBLOC
WAREBPAR
WAREBSTO
WAREBSUB
WARECLNT
WAREPART
WARESCLN
WARESPAR
WARESSAL
WARESUPL

*WAREPROC.PRG is a procedure file that contains the files listed beneath it. The procedure file is used to save space and boost program speed.

C3.3

Indexed and Required Fields: Dynamic Inventory Management Program

Indexes		Required Input Fields
Warebuy	—Part # + Purchase date	Part #
	—Stock #	Supplier #
	—Location	
	—Supplier #	
Waresale	—Sale	Part #
	—Customer #	Customer #
	—Part #	
Wareclnt	—Client #	Client #
	—Client Name	Client Name
Waresupl	—Supplier	Supplier #
	—Supplier Name	Supplier Name
Warepart	—Part #	Part #
	—Part Name	Part Name

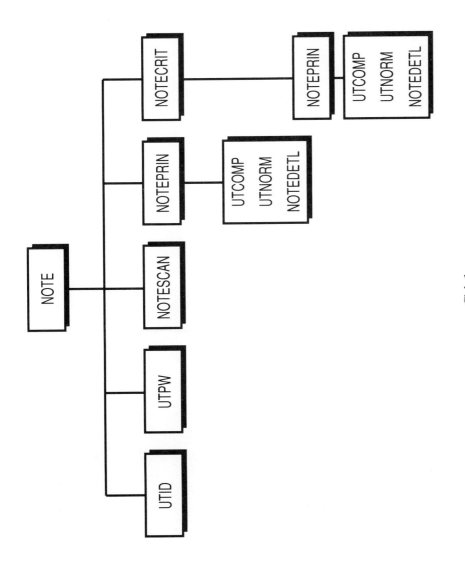

C4.1
Program Tree: Note Card

C4.2

Required Files: Note Card Program

Database (.DBF)	Program (.PRG)
NOTE	NOTE
UTID	NOTEPROC*
UTPW	Consists of:
	—NOTECRIT
	—NOTEDETL
	—NOTEPRIN
Format (.FMT)	—NOTESCAN
NOTEDISP	UTBLKDEL
NOTEEDIT	UTCOMP
NOTETEXT	UTDCRYPT
	UTECRYPT
Report (.FRM)	UTEXIT
	UTFACE
NOTESUB	UTTD
NOTESUM	UTNORM
NOTETEXT	UTPACK
NOTETOP	UTPW
NOTETPSJ	

* Noteproc.prg is a procedure file that contains the files listed beneath it. The procedure file is used to save space and boost program speed.

C4.3

Indexed and Required Fields: Note Card Program

Indexes	Required Input Fields
- Topic + Subject	None Required
- Subject	
- Code1	
- Code2	
- Order	

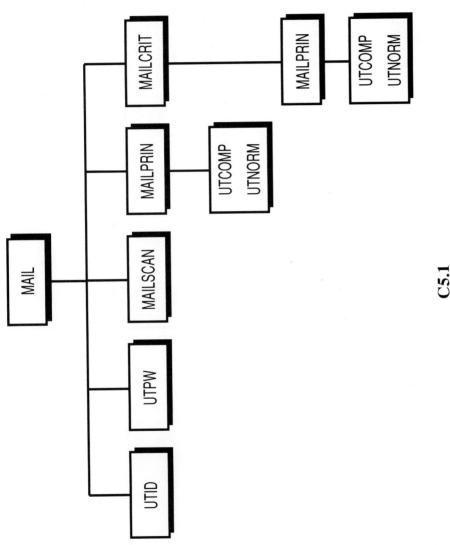

C5.1

Program Tree: Mailing List Management Program

C5.2

Required Files: Mailing List Management Program.

Database (.DBF)	Program (.PRG)
MAIL	MAIL
UTID	MAILCRIT
UTPW	MAILPRIN
	MAILSCAN
	UTCOMP
Format (.FMT)	UTDCRYPT
	UTECRYPT
MAILDFLT	UTEXIT
MAILDISP	UTFACE
MAILEDIT	UTID
MAILINP	UTNORM
	UTPACK
Report (.FRM)	UTPW
MAILDETL	
MAILSUM	
Label (.LBL)	
MAILCHES	
MAILONE	
MAILTHRE	
MAILWIDE	

C5.3

Indexed and Required Fields: Mailing List Management Program.

Indexes	Required Input Fields
-Last Name + First Name	Last Name
-Company	or
-State + City	Company
-Zip	

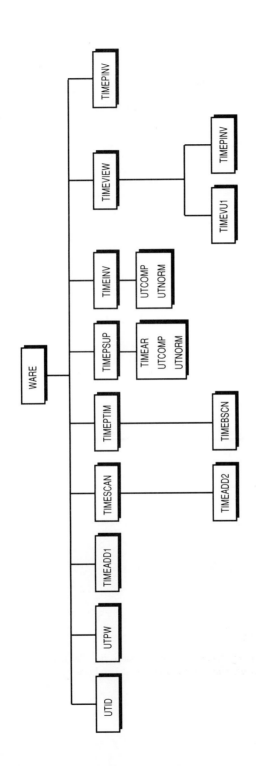

C6.1
Program Tree: Time Billing Program

C6.2

Required Files: Time Billing Program.

Database (.DBF)	Program (.PRG)
TIMEBILL	TIME
TIMECLNT	TIMEVIEW
TIMEEMPL	
TIMEPROJ	TIMEPROC*
TIMETASK	Contains
UTID	—TIMEADD1
UTPW	—TIMEADD2
	—TTMEAR
Format (.FMT)	—TIMEBSCN
	—TIMEINV
TIMEBDIS	—TIMEPINV
TIMEBED	—TIMEPSUP
TTMECDIS	—TIMEPTIM
TIMECED	—TIMESCAN
TIMEINP	—TIMEVUE
TIMEDISP	
TIMEEDIS	UTCOMP
TIMEED	UTDCRYPT
TIMEEINP	UTECRYPT
TIMEPDIS	UTEXIT
TIMEPED	UTFACE
TIMEPINP	UTID
TIMETDIS	UTNORM
TIMETED	UTPACK
TIMETINP	UTPACK
TIMEVIEW	UTPW

Report (.FRM)

TIMEBCLN
TIMEBEMP
TIMEBILL
TIMEBPRO
TIMEBTAS
TIMECLNT
TIMEEMPL
TIMEPROJ
TTMETASK

* TIMEPROC.PRG is a procedure file that contains the files listed beneath it. The procedure file is used to save space and boost program speed.

C6.3

Indexed and Required Fields: Time Billing Program.

Indexes		Required Input Fields
Timebill	- Client # - Employee # - Project # - Task # - Invoice # - Billing Date	Client # Employee # Project # Task #
Timeempl	- Employee # - Employee Name	Employee # Employee Name
Timeclnt	- Client # - Client Name	Client # Client Name
Timeproj	- Project # - Project Name	Project # Project Name
Timetask	- Task # - Task Name	Task # Task Name

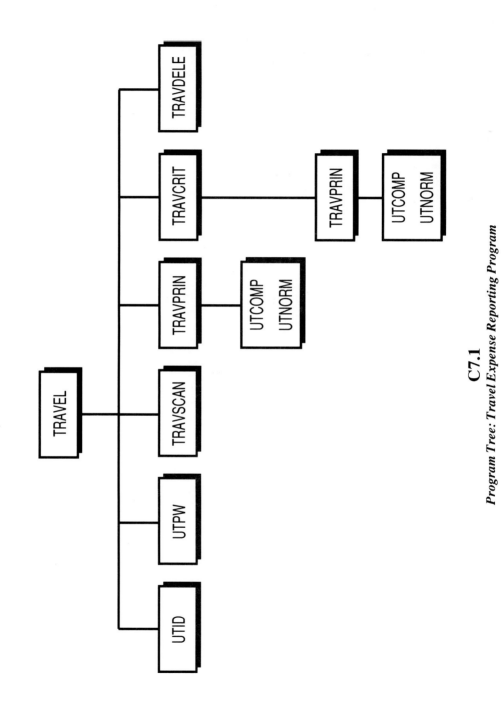

C7.1
Program Tree: Travel Expense Reporting Program

C7.2

Required Files: Travel Expense Reporting Program

Database (.DBF)	Program (.PRG)
TRAVEL	TRAVEL
UTID	TRAVPROC
UTPW	TRAVCRIT
	TRAVDELE
Format (.FMT)	TRAVPRIN
	TRAVSCAN
TRAVDISP	
TRAVEDIT	UTCOMP
TRAVINP	UTDCRYPT
	UTECRYPT
Report (.FRM)	UTEXIT
	UTFACE
TRAVBUD	UTID
TRAVCLNT	UTNORM
TRAVDEPT	UTPACK
TRAVTRAV	UTPW

C7.3

Indexed and Required Fields: Travel Expense Reporting Program

Indexes	Required Input Fields
- Employee + Date	Employee
- Client + Date	or
- Department + Budget + Date	Client
- Budget + Date	

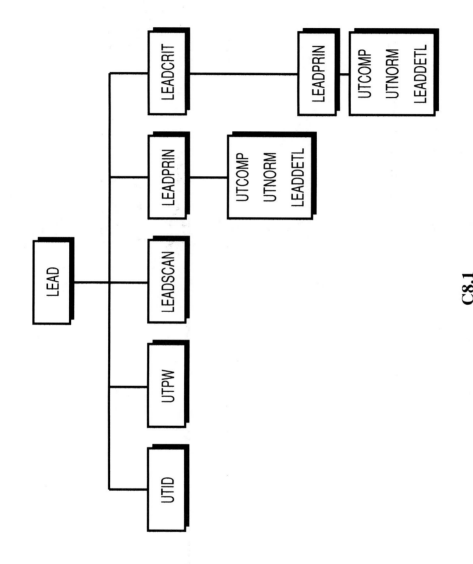

C8.1
Program Tree: Sales Lead Management Program

C8.2

Required Files: Sales Lead Management Program

Database (.DBF)	Program (.PRG)
LEAD	LEAD
UTID	
UTPW	LEADPROC*
	Consists of
	—LEADCRIT
Format (.FMT)	—LEADDETL
	—LEADPRIN
LEADDISP	—LEADSCAN
LEADEDIT	
LEADINP	UTCOMP
	UTDCRYPT
Report (.FRM)	UTECRYPT
	UTEXIT
LEADREP	UTFACE
LEADSOUR	UTID
LEADSUM	UTNORM
	UTPACK
	UTPW

* Leadproc.prg is a procedure file that contains the files listed beneath it. The procedure file is used to save space and boost program speed.

C8.3

Indexed and Required Fields: Sales Lead Management

Indexes	Required Input Fields
- Lead Type + Source Code	Item
- Source Code	or
- Item	Client
- Model	
- Region	
- Client	
- epresentative	

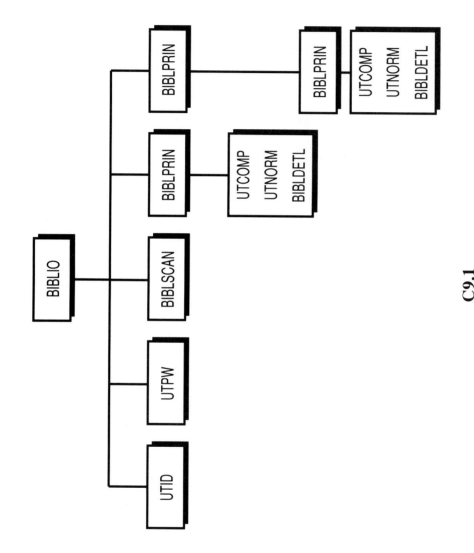

C9.1
Program Tree: Bibliography Program

C9.2

Required Files: Bibliography Program.

Database (.DBF)	Program (.PRG)
BIBL	
UTID	BIBLI0
UTPW	
	BIBLPROC*
Format (.FMT)	Consists of:
	—BIBLCRIT
BIBLDISP	—BIBLDETL
BIBLEDIT	—BIBLPRIN
BIBLTEXT	—BIBLSCAN
Report (.FRM)	UTCOMP
	UTDCRYPT
BIBLBIBL	UTECRYPT
BIBLFOOT	UTEXIT
BIBLSUBJ	UTFACE
BIBLSUM	UTID
BIBLTEXT	UTNORM
BIBLTOP	UTPACK
BIBLTPSJ	UTPW
	Memo Files (.DBT)
	BIBL

* BIBLPROC.PRG is a procedure file that contains the files listed beneath it. The procedure file is used to save space and boost program speed.

C9.3

Indexed and Required Files: Bibliography Program.

Indexes	Required Input Fields
- Topic + Subject	None Required
- Subject	
- Authors	
- Title	
- Order	
- Footnote	

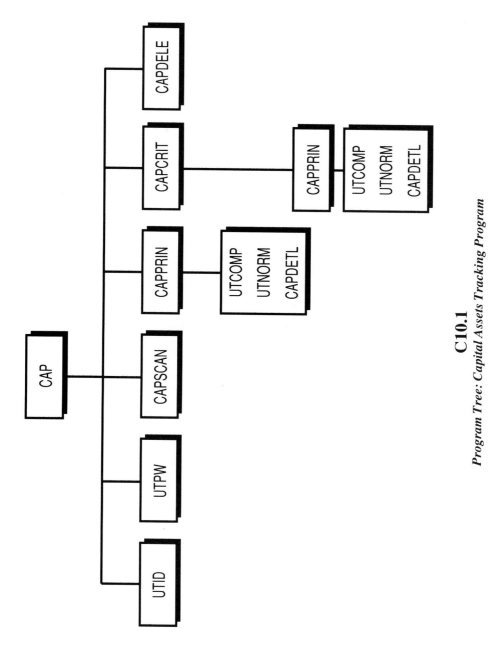

C10.1

Program Tree: Capital Assets Tracking Program

C10.2

Required Files: Capital Assets Tracking Program.

Database (.DBF)	Program (.PRG)
CAP	CAP
UTID	CAPPROC*
UTPW	Consists of:
	—CAPCRIT
Format (.FMT)	—CAPDELE
	—CAPDEPR
CAPDISP	—CAPDETL
CAPEDIT	—CAPPRIN
CAPINP	—CAPSCAN
Report (.FRM)	UTCOMP
	UTDCRYPT
CAPDEPR	UTECRYPT
CAPPDET	UTEXIT
CAPDPSUM	UTFACE
CAPSUM	UTID
	UTNORM
	UTPACK

* CAPPROC.PRG is a procedure file that contains the files listed beneath it. The procedure file is used to save space and boost program speed.

C10.3

Indexed and Required Fields: Capital Assets Tracking Program.

Indexes	Required Input Fields
- Asset # or	Asset #
- Asset Name	Asset Name
- Department + Budget	
- Budget	
- Codel + Code2	
- Code2 + Codel	
- Location	

WordTech Systems, Inc.
License Agreement

I. Definitions

A. "WORDTECH" shall mean WordTech Systems, Inc., P.O. Box 1747, Orinda, California 94563, U.S.A.

B. "CUSTOMER" shall mean the original customer, either an individual or a company.

C. "PROGRAM" shall mean the software and related manuals and materials supplied in this package.

D. "COMPUTER" shall mean the single computer on which this program is used.

E. "LICENSE" shall mean this Agreement and the rights and obligations created hereunder by the United States Copyright Law and California Law.

F. "SYSTEMS SUPPORT LIBRARY" shall refer to a set of copyrighted WordTech Systems,Inc. language subroutines, provided with some PROGRAMS, a portion of which must be linked to and become a part of a CUSTOMER program for that program to run on the COMPUTER.

G. "COMPILER" shall mean any WORDTECH PROGRAM containing a SYSTEMS SUPPORT LIBRARY.

H. "NETWORK FILE SERVER MODULE" shall mean any WORDTECH PROGRAM which is loaded on the file server of a Local Area Network for the purpose of providing concurrency control for WORDTECH PROGRAMS or for other network utility functions.

I. "UNIX MODULE" shall mean any WORDTECH PROGRAM which is loaded on a multiuser UNIX system for the purpose of running WORDTECH PROGRAMS or other UNIX applications from multiple user stations.

II. License

WORDTECH grants to CUSTOMER the right to use this copy of the PROGRAM on a single COMPUTER at a single location as long as CUSTOMER complies with the terms of this LICENSE. WORDTECH reserves the right to terminate this LICENSE if CUSTOMER violates any provisions hereof and, in the event of such termination, CUSTOMER agrees to return the PROGRAM to WORDTECH. The PROGRAM is the sole and exclusive property of WORDTECH. CUSTOMER ownership is limited to the diskette(s) purchased. CUSTOMER agrees to make no more than TWO (2) copies of the software for archival purposes and further agrees to label said copies with all information included on the original diskette label(s). In the event that CUSTOMER uses the PROGRAM simultaneously on more than one COMPUTER, CUSTOMER agrees to request from WORDTECH and to pay for licenses for additional user copies. A sealed copy of the PROGRAM is supplied with the documentation. By the act of opening the package within which the program diskette(s) is sealed, CUSTOMER subscribes to and agrees to the terms of this licensing agreement.

III. Network File Server and UNIX Modules

As an exception to paragraph II, NETWORK FILE SERVER and UNIX MODULE CUSTOMERS are granted the right to load NETWORK FILE SERVER and UNIX MODULE files from the file server and run those files on any workstation attached to the file server upon which the NETWORK FILE SERVER or UNIX MODULE is loaded.

IV. Transfer and Reproduction

CUSTOMER agrees to take all reasonable steps and to exercise due diligence to protect the PROGRAM from unauthorized reproduction, publication, disclosure, or distribution. Unauthorized transfer and/or reproduction of these materials may be a crime, subjecting CUSTOMER to civil and criminal prosecution. CUSTOMER may not transfer any copy of the PROGRAM to any other person without the prior written consent of WORDTECH. WORDTECH reserves the right to revoke this LICENSE and/or to seek any other legal remedies to which it is entitled should these conditions be violated.

V. Composite Programs

As an exception to Paragraph IV, COMPILER CUSTOMERS are granted the right to include compiled portions of the SYSTEMS SUPPORT LIBRARY in CUSTOMER developed Composite Programs, and to use, distribute, and license such Composite Programs to third parties without payment of any further license fee. CUSTOMER shall, however, include in such Composite Programs, and on the exterior label of every diskette, a copyright notice in this form: "Portions of this program, Copyright 1984, 1985, 1986, 1987, 1988, 1989, WordTech Systems, Inc." As an express condition to the use of the SYSTEMS SUPPORT LIBRARY, CUSTOMER agrees to indemnify and hold WORDTECH harmless from any and all claims by CUSTOMER and/or third parties arising out of the use of Composite Programs.

VI. Limited Warranty

THE PROGRAM IS SOLD "AS IS" WITHOUT WARRANTY AS TO PERFORMANCE, MERCHANTABILITY, OR FITNESS FOR ANY PARTICULAR PURPOSE. THE ENTIRE RISK AS TO THE RESULTS AND PERFORMANCE OF THIS PROGRAM IS ASSUMED BY CUSTOMER.

HOWEVER, WORDTECH WARRANTS THE MAGNETIC DISKETTE(S) ON WHICH THE PROGRAM IS RECORDED TO BE FREE FROM DEFECTS IN MATERIALS AND FAULTY WORKMANSHIP UNDER NORMAL USE FOR A PERIOD OF NINETY (90) DAYS FROM THE DATE OF PURCHASE. IF DURING THIS NINETY-DAY PERIOD THE DISKETTE(S) SHOULD BECOME DEFECTIVE, THEY MAY BE RETURNED TO WORDTECH FOR REPLACEMENT WITHOUT CHARGE.

IN ADDITION, WORDTECH WARRANTS THE PRINTED MATERIAL(S) TO BE FREE FROM MATERIAL DEFECTS FOR NINETY (90) DAYS FROM THE DATE OF PURCHASE. IF DURING THIS NINETY-DAY PERIOD THE PRINTED MATERIALS ARE FOUND TO BE DEFECTIVE, THEY MAY BE RETURNED TO WORDTECH FOR REPLACEMENT WITHOUT CHARGE.

IN ADDITION, WORDTECH WARRANTS THE SOFTWARE TO BE FREE OF SIGNIFICANT ERRORS THAT MAKE IT UNUSABLE FOR NINETY (90) DAYS FROM THE DATE OF PURCHASE. IN THE EVENT SUCH ERRORS ARE FOUND, WORDTECH WILL ATTEMPT TO CORRECT THEM, OR TO HELP CUSTOMER AVOID THEM, WITH EFFORTS WORDTECH BELIEVES SUITABLE TO THE PROBLEM OR, AT WORDTECH'S OPTION, AUTHORIZE A REFUND OF THE LICENSE FEE.

CUSTOMER'S SOLE AND EXCLUSIVE REMEDY IN THE EVENT OF A DEFECT IS EXPRESSLY LIMITED TO THE ABOVE PROVISIONS. WORDTECH MAKES NO WARRANTY AGAINST MATERIAL THAT HAS BEEN LOST, STOLEN, OR DAMAGED BY ACCIDENT, MISUSE, OR UNAUTHORIZED MODIFICATION.

WORDTECH MAKES NO OTHER WARRANTY, EXPRESS OR IMPLIED, TO CUSTOMER OR ANY OTHER ENTITY OR PERSON. SPECIFICALLY, WORDTECH MAKES NO WARRANTY THAT THE SOFTWARE IS FIT FOR A PARTICULAR PURPOSE. ANY IMPLIED WARRANTY OF MERCHANTABILITY IS LIMITED TO THE NINETY-DAY DURATION OF THIS LIMITED WARRANTY AND IS OTHERWISE EXPRESSLY AND SPECIFICALLY DISCLAIMED.

WORDTECH WILL NOT BE LIABLE FOR SPECIAL, INCIDENTAL, CONSEQUENTIAL, INDIRECT, OR OTHER SIMILAR DAMAGES, EVEN IF WORDTECH OR WORDTECH'S AGENT HAS BEEN ADVISED OF THE POSSIBILITY OF SUCH DAMAGES. This means WORDTECH is not responsible or liable for damages or costs incurred as a result of loss of time, loss of data, loss of profits or revenue, or loss of use of the software, or software created by the software, or any other losses whatsoever. In addition, WORDTECH is not responsible or liable for damages or costs incurred in connection with obtaining substitute software, claims by others, inconvenience, or similar costs.

IN NO EVENT WILL WORDTECH'S LIABILITY FOR ANY DAMAGES TO CUSTOMER OR ANY OTHER ENTITY OR PERSON EVER EXCEED THE PRICE PAID FOR THE LICENSE TO USE THE SOFTWARE, REGARDLESS OF ANY FORM OF THE CLAIM.

SOME STATES DO NOT ALLOW THE EXCLUSION OR LIMITATION OF INCIDENTAL OR CONSEQUENTIAL DAMAGES, SO THE ABOVE LIMITATIONS MIGHT NOT APPLY TO YOU. THIS WARRANTY GIVES YOU SPECIFIC LEGAL RIGHTS, AND YOU MAY ALSO HAVE OTHER RIGHTS WHICH VARY FROM STATE TO STATE. CUSTOMER and WORDTECH agree that the PROGRAM is not intended as "Consumer Goods" under state or federal warranty laws.

VII. Miscellaneous

WORDTECH maintains a policy of ongoing updates and product improvement. Provided CUSTOMER has previously returned the signed limited warranty registration card, WORDTECH shall provide CUSTOMER with either copies of updated material or notification of availability and price schedules where appropriate. The PROGRAM specifications and features are subject to change without notice.

In the event legal action is brought by either CUSTOMER or WORDTECH to enforce the terms of the licensing agreement, the prevailing party shall be entitled to recover reasonable attorney's fees and expenses in addition to any other relief deemed appropriate by the court.

This agreement shall represent the only agreement between CUSTOMER and WORDTECH, and it may not be modified by the representations of anyone unless a written amendment has been signed by a corporate officer of WordTech Systems, Inc.

WordTech Systems, Inc.